Existence.

Addressing Urban Skepticism & the Purpose of Life

Dr. Alfonse Javed

ANM
publishers

Existence.

by Dr. Alfonse Javed

ISBN: 978-0-9908372-0-6 Paperback

Published by:

Advancing Native Missions
P.O. Box 5303 • Charlottesville, VA 22905
www.AdvancingNativeMissions.com

Contents

Introduction

We raise our eyebrows at non-conformists because they live a lifestyle that is "anti-society" yet, in reality, the non-conformists themselves are conforming to something-a certain set of unspoken rules. Likewise, we all are in some way non-conformists; we all despise the set rules and regulations, yet we live by another set of rules. In life, our demands and needs are always pushing us to adapt to something that is only acceptable under undeniable necessity. History is a cruel witness to the fact that, before necessity, even the most highly decorated and moral individuals will shamelessly surrender. In general, regardless of our personal preferences, we are destined to compromise. Those who do not compromise become the outlaws. It has been said before: those who do not bend will break. However, as intellectual beings we should be questioning the social norm. What is said will be said again; time passes and will continue to pass with the same pace it always has. If you can't write history, then to be part of it. Whether you will be remembered by one or by one million, it is better to be remembered by some than none at all.

This book is an open challenge to our intellects, belief systems, ethics and values. It is a challenge to reassess and take a second look at life, its purpose and value. Are you happy? Whatever the answer is, the question you should be asking is "Why?" Will your happiness last? How long do you expect it to last? Perhaps it would be in the best interest of humans to simply not bother with how long happiness will last, but to enjoy every moment of life. Nevertheless, life is made of a multitude of moments; some happy and some not.

Blaise Pascal quipped, "All of humanity's problems stem from man's inability to sit quietly in a room alone," a discipline that invites us to look deep inside and search some of the most difficult questions of our time. Why life? Where does it come from, and where does it go? What is my purpose on this earth? Why is there suffering and pain? Is there another intelligent life in the universe? Is there a God? Many of us believe in evil (Satan) before we believe in good (God).

Part One
Life, Love and Logic

Chapter I
The Philosophy of Life

N ew York City has everything. Every New Yorker, whether they are poor, middle class, rich, or ultra rich, loves this city and is proud of it; but, at the same time they complain about it all. This is just a part of being New Yorkers; we are an opinionated people. We have opinions about everything, even about nothing. NYC is considered the center of the world because of its financial districts, showbiz attractions, politics, ethnic diversity and much more. Here you find Broadway theaters, drama, art, technology, The New York Times, history, architecture, innovation, pizza, bagels, and everything in between. New York has some of the most brilliant minds in the world. Columbia University and New York University are two of many other excellent schools in the city who invite and train the international community right here. Here the United Nations and its global leadership come together to find ways to fight hunger, promote peace, and ensure the safety of life in the world. The focus remains on life.

What makes New York City exceptional is the people of New York, diverse in every possible way, yet, as New Yorkers, so different from the rest of the world. The intellectual contribution of New Yorkers is not a secret; we all think alike yet, differently. If you want me to agree with you on a point, do not tell me, but wait patiently. I will come to my own conclusion, or to none. It goes like this; if you give me the conclusion and want me to believe it, more often than not, it will never happen. The free spirit of skepticism among New Yorkers demands a high level of intellectual respect. What makes New Yorkers unique in their thought process is their ability to think through, analyze and not take anyone's word for anything, not their friends, family members, the government, politicians, or any authority on any subject. Nothing is taken at face value, but it is received with a great deal of skepticism. What is in it for me? This is a question that even children will ask in New York. When it comes to the philosophy of life, we define life in many ways and discuss its forms in great length, but we respectfully disagree with each other. Do you think like a New Yorker? Philosophically speaking, life exists in the mind, heart, and soul; yet once a body is gone, their life is sustained in their values and respect and lives on in the thoughts of others Their soul is set free to continue its life in another age and time that we call eternity. The question about life is the most ancient, complicated, and investigated in all fields. Life is spread over the unknown span of time.

One way to look at the brutal reality of time is: It has been said before that time heals all wounds. We use the phrase to express that when you are hurting physically or emotionally it takes time to heal. So, when you have been hurt, in time the pain will go away. Will it? I raise this question to seek truth, not to conceal it. Truth shall set us all free. Open this up to your assessment. Here is one response, "I lost my husband over 20 year ago, and my son 19 months later. I know that it is true, but there is still a feeling of loss. The pain is less and the hole in your heart is a little smaller." let us consider the example of a soldier who was severely injured in the line of duty 13 years ago, who still feels the presence of an amputated limb. Can he say that the time has healed his wounds? How about your own painful experiences that can never be subdued? The time does not heal our wounds; it is the people around us who help us to get through it. Our perspective on our struggles changes over the time as we realize that we are neither the first nor the last one to such struggles. This is precisely why sharing is important.

What I have learned in the hours of my troubles and trials is only valuable to me alone if I keep it to myself, but, if I expose it to others, it will benefit everyone because we all share the same struggles. Time does not heal, it simply subdues. Perhaps the intensity one understood and felt at first may reduce to moderation, but it will be an unbreakable part of the very soul as long as one lives. I would say it again; it is the sharing and acknowledging of our pain that helps. When it comes to suffering and pain or hurtful memories of the past, some matters are simply out of our reach, as for the others, we need simply to look back and see from where we have come. Along the way, we have learned incomparable lessons that one lifetime cannot provide.

Our Environment and An Experiment: If you are performing an experiment under the same circumstances without any variation, in the environment, location or temperature, you will likely retrieve the same results each time you run that experiment. The outcomes of one's actions in life can be predetermined if one's life functions as an experiment and if, from day one, the surroundings act as a lab in which all variations that have been tested on other subjects first. It may only be circumvented entirely if the subject willfully accepts the conditions he/she is placed in, considering this is how it is and how it was and how it will be, leaving no room for questioning or pondering the possibility of alternatives. As much as it sounds like a surreptitious affair, or a conspiracy against human life, the answers have always been there. As the sand is scattered on the seashores, and the stars are spread all over the sky, in the same way we find scattered evidence all over that is inviting us in to tame our ontological thirst and to find truth. The earth is old, but the world is new; every passing moment, the creeping noises from the rotten joints of this earth give us one challenge and one challenge alone: make the time to rethink God, values and life.

Continuity of Life: Life is. It never has been a matter of was. Among all that is seen and unseen, thought and unthinkable, life is the most ancient entity that one can witness over and over again. It has seen many forms and shapes, but life itself has no beginning and no end. A continual length of life is impossible to determine, comprehend or measure. The beauty of life resides only in itself; the outlook and body it wears is merely a distorted reflection of the true beauty it possesses. It sustains itself, what is precious to it, and that which is more precious than anything else, survival. So an unbroken relation between sustaining and surviving life is forced to guard itself in order to preserve the next cycle of life. To itself alone it owes everything, including the emergence of one life from another. Thus, it jumps from one form or shape to another in a tireless loop that has always been there and will always be. This is precisely why people throughout the generations have studied life, but no one has been able to contain it in a bottle. Rather, life has always been an independent entity-self existing, self sustaining, and self emerging.

If you examine closely, you will find that everything visible and invisible is the result of self sustainable and unimaginable vastness of some living source. It would not be wrong to call such source the parent life because it is the source of all life. It has its dominion on the earth and on many unknown places that are much greater and older far superior and matchless. Beyond our reach and imaginations the parent life has stretched its sovereignty. The source of the parent life is life itself; thus it bestows only what it graciously considers to be given little by little, only to take it back. Subsequently, one life comes and another moves away, never to be distinguished and extinguished. Death is a word of the mortals, but in the realms of immortals, no dictionary holds such a word or its description because it is useless and meaningless as is lifetime. The eternity of life is easy to understand from a religious viewpoint, where the God figure, with no beginning and no end, is life and is the life-giver subsequently leaving no option for mortals to live in the same body once the divine decree calls their life back to its origin. Intellectual beings have always challenged the religious notion of life in God, yet they have never ruled out the possibility. Therefore, more questions and a fair understanding of all possibilities (including the possibility of whether the divine hand is behind life and in life), has never ever dismissed.

Life is not subject to time, yet time most certainly abounds as a servant of life. The reality of life is such as the ocean. A multitude of drops, that together have the power to eliminate anything, aside from life itself. Life has the power to create and destroy, build and tear down; it can neither be detained nor executed. It lies out in a memory or in an image; it wears us down from time to time. No environment can be hostile to it because it is eternal, unlike the environment itself. No life is more or less valuable than another, since it is the part of the same parent life. Therefore even if a life is considered to be more precious than another simply because of skin color or body type at the end of the day, it is one and the same. We may foolishly divide life, but life doesn't divide itself.

Chapter 2
The Relationship of Choices and Questions

Imagine living in New York City, with an abundance of every-thing, people and services. Every day, people of different ethnicities and backgrounds consume and randomly choose from available services, not because they have to, but because they choose to do so. We live in a fast paced world. We want things, and we want them right away; we pick and choose as we wish. Whether you are looking to purchase a sweater or a taco, the mass of choices will certainly overwhelm you in this city. You can choose something to wear from all kinds of famous name brands on 5th Avenue in Manhattan, or travel four avenues over for hundreds of choices of ethnic restaurants on 9th Avenue. Even if you experience all of them, this is only the beginning of the diversity that this city has to offer.

Choices: The bombardment of options and choices is inter-twined with the culture of instant gratification that has domi-nated our society for the last few decades. Both feed off of each other, thus making the idea of consumerism an acceptable social norm. Because of this, we end up feeling the need to buy and buy, even when we do not need to. In many ways, fast technolog-ical advancement has contributed to this phenomenon of instant gratification. We can have food delivered in 15 minutes, have our groceries delivered the same day (a recent ad that was in the subway mocked the traditional way of shopping by comparing it to the "fossil way of life"), and we can stream thousands of movies and shows instantly through the internet- all because the technology exists to do so. We should be thankful for the advancement of technology, yet we must be very careful.

The Pew Research Center's Internet & American Life Project sums up a recent study on young people's hyper-connected lives with what sounds like a prescription drug warning: "Negative effects include a need for instant gratification and loss of patience."[1] Other studies have shown that the span of our patience has been reduced drastically. A study of 6.7 million internet users shows that after just two seconds, the subjects started losing interest. After five seconds, 25 percent of the subjects have already given up.

The new culture of instant gratification negates the true meanings of a choice. One can define choice philosophically, as a corollary of the proposition of free will—i.e., the ability to voluntarily decide to perform one of several possible acts or to avoid action entirely. An ethical choice involves ascribing qualities such as right or wrong, good or bad, better or worse to alternatives.[2]

So there is a direct link between our choices, the culture we live in, and our patience level. If you concentrate on your behavior, you will find that your choices are not selected from unlimited boundaries; rather, they are confined to the boundaries of availability (your knowledge of the available options). Your instincts tell you to choose from your available options. You can never even attempt to think about an item in the first place if it is not on your list of options. (However, that is something that should be treasured by all humans because whenever someone tries to think about the non-existing option, the result always ends up being innovating and inventing. We call these extraordinary options.) On a greater scale the choices are made for you. You are simply choosing from the options that were chosen for you. On the other hand, generally speaking, the more options you have (or at least the more options of which you are aware), the more difficult the decision becomes. If the available options are equally valuable and desirable, it would be an even harder choice. Sometimes, when a person makes a choice from equally important items, dissatisfaction is inevitable because of the doubt regarding whether or not one's decision was the correct one. Therefore, our decision and our choices are co-dependent on each other. Are they not?

Questions are the reflection of our inner being. We are naturally curious people. We ask questions regardless of their relevance or level of significance. Also, our answers are largely shaped by how we phrase our question.

Questions: There is a very basic principle in the formation of a question. Our mind and our will are always seeking to determine the best scenario possible to accommodate our being's desire to be satisfied. Our subconscious desire to discover the truth, is subjective based on our own individual bias and it leads to the knowledge of our own being. If questioning is not the sole basis of knowledge that a person gains, then at the very least it plays a constitutive role.[3]

When we were young, we asked questions just to get to know our surroundings and our relationship to them. As we grew, our understanding about our surroundings expanded. Whether a question is asked for personal knowledge, to satisfy one's own curiosity or to benefit others, they are always at the root of the unknown. The beauty of human curiosity is that the more you know, the more you want to know. When it comes to knowledge and information, the sky is the limit. However, most of the answers to our questions are directly connected to our own being; thus, when we are still and willing to open our mind to less noticeable things that surround us, we discover that the answers to many of our questions were always there. Some of the best thinkers in the history of humankind were struck by knowledge not in a highly reputed school or laboratory, but in very ordinary places simply by paying attention to the things that were around them. For Heraclitus, it was a river; for the Buddha, a tree; for Archimedes, a bathtub; for Socrates, a marketplace and a dinner party; for Aristotle, two royal palaces; for Descartes, a heating stove; for Isaac Newton, an apple tree; and for Ludwig Wittgenstein, a don's room with a fire and poker.[4]

It is good to raise questions, but questions will not benefit you or anyone else much if you are not open to hearing the answer. Academically speaking, we teach young children to find an answer through raising questions, and there are two types of questions; thin questions and thick questions. One can find the answers of the thin questions within the proximity of his/her known knowledge; for thick questions, you must consult outside resources. What are some of the questions that you have? Where do you find hope? Does your life have purpose and significance? Is there any peace in these troubled times? What is this life about? Is this all there is? If you desire to receive genuine answers to your questions, then I invite you on a journey where you must unarm yourself from all personal biases and let knowledge and reasoning take its course.

Endnotes

1   Janna Anderson and Lee Rainie, "Main Findings: Teens, technology, and human potential in 2020," February 29, 2012, PewReseach Internet Project. http://www.pewinternet.org/2012/02/29/main-findings-teens-technology-and-human-potential-in-2020/ (accessed June 26, 2014).

2   Encyclopaedia Britannica, 8th ed., s.v. "Internet." Chicago: Encyclopaedia Britannica, 2014. http://www.britannica.com/EBchecked/topic/113978/choice (accessed June 26, 2014).

3   Nick Turnbull, "Dewey's philosophy of questioning: science, practical reason and democracy," History of the Human Sciences 21. no.1 (2008): 49-75.

4   Os Guinness, Unspeakable: Facing up to the challenge of evil (New York: HarperCollins Publishers, 2006), 34.

Chapter 3
The Marriage of Religion and Science

I believe that most questioning in human history occurred due to the fact that we find ourselves left alone. Questions such as, "Is there any other being out there other than us?" "What is the purpose of my life?" "Why life?" "Why death?" "Why suffering, pain, and disease?" Throughout history, finding a way to escape death and our curiosity about what is after death has driven humankind to rely on medicine, science, and spirituality for answers.

The East offered religions and reliance on gods; philosophy and theology, whether mistakenly or intentionally, became the currency of intellectual realms. The West dragged barely breathing civilization from the dark ages to enlightenment, shedding a new light on rational by making it all about science and technology. Subsequently, the idea that something must be proven scientifically in order to be true became the new social norm for thinking. The truth was reduced to the level of relevance.

Junction: The idea of death is so frightening that from ancient times it has been discussed as a philosophy, a belief, and an enemy. Throughout the centuries, many have tried to escape the reality of death, but, regardless of their denial, when their time on earth was over, they were gone whether or not they had left any footsteps on human history. The human search and desire to beat death and find immortality is not an ancient myth, but a reality of the past and the present. This is one junction where both the East (philosophical and theological rationale) and the West (scientific rationale) agree; basically, that whatever works should be tried. For example, in the modern practice of Cryonics, people beyond the reach of today's medicine are being stored at very low temperatures in the hope that future medicine is able to revive and cure them. Sixty-three signatories encompassing all disciplines relevant to cryonics, including Biology, Cryobiology, Neuroscience, Physical Science, Nanotechnology and Computing, Ethics and Theology, published an open letter stating:

> *To whom it may concern,*
>
> *Cryonics is a legitimate science-based endeavor that seeks to preserve human beings, especially the human brain, by means of the best technology available. Future technologies for resuscitation can be envisioned that involve molecular repair by nanomedicine, highly advanced computation, detailed control of cell growth, and tissue regeneration.*
>
> *With a view toward these developments, there is a credible possibility that cryonics performed under the best conditions achievable today can preserve sufficient neurological information to permit eventual restoration of a person to full health.[5]*
>
> *The rights of people who choose cryonics are important, and should be respected.*

An unrealistic hope but very sincere question is, "When our time is up, can we really resist?"

Life: We are people with needs. We are bombarded by choices and we have to make those choices one way or another. Some choices have more or less value than others, some have temporary consequences and others permanent, some last for a while and others forever.

Such everlasting choices can alter the path of your life. Is it absurd to ask the question "What are the choices that can affect our life for eternity?" In 1892, a piece was published in the British Fiend, a Quaker magazine, in which George MacDonald said: "Never tell a child you have a soul. Teach him, 'You are a soul; you have a body.'" If that is the case, then which is more important, body or soul? We worry too much about the body and forget to plan for our souls. When does life begin? This is an ongoing debate in our society, but when it comes to death we can all agree that it means the end of life. If life is a time of celebration, then death is a time of mourning. Life and death are two ends of the same string. Where there is life, there is also death. Thus, ignoring such an important subject will not help anyone.

Death: Death is a subject that is so crucial to humankind yet discussed so little, in society and in religious circles. In the Bible, it appears 372 times. Wherever there is a mention of life, you will also find death. As soon we open the Bible, we see God busy creating everything and bringing forth both light and life. However, by the time we approach Genesis 2:17, God is already talking about death as a consequence of Adam and Eve's disobedience. In George MacDonald's words "All that is not God is death."

The phenomenon of death is that it will be the last thing every human being will taste on this earth, and this fact is a challenge that has left humans vulnerable before nature. Although death is a natural process of life, it is the most difficult thing we have to deal with. It includes both the person who is dying and the one who sees a loved one dying. The idea of losing our loved ones is not unique to humankind, but coping with it sucks the life out of us. We can never be prepared enough to cope with a loved one's death. It is the gruesome reality of life that our days are numbered, as are those of our loved ones.

There is an appointed time for everything. And there is a time for every event under heaven. "A time to be born, and a time to die" (Ecclesiastes 3:1-2). Is there anyone who can find disagreement with this wisdom? I seriously doubt it.

Endnotes

5   Institute for Evidence-Based Cryonics, Scientists' Open Letter on Cryonics, http://www.evidencebasedcryonics.org/scientists-open-letter-on-cryonics/ (accessed June 23, 2014).

Chapter 4
The Logic of Love and Care

Death itself is not the issue; the true horror of death is the fear of losing someone that we care about. We are social beings, and it seems that our very chemistry has built us to crumble in the face of love, care, and the need for the company of others. Sometimes we do not demonstrate this innate love for the other as we should, but everyone, even the worst human being, loves and cares about something or someone.

Separation: It is because of this very nature that the thought of permanent separation from loved ones makes us queasy. If we could, we would not let our loved ones die, and, because of the same fear of separation, we do not want to die either. Some time ago, my youngest sister gave birth to a baby girl, and for once everyone was happy. The whole family forgot their personal issues, and they were celebrating the birth of little Ariala. But, suddenly, it was discovered that my sister, Ariala's mother, was in critical condition at the hospital, and the joy went out the window. Tears, weeping, and prayers for her healing replaced the joyous moment. The thought of losing her was horrifying to all of us, to the point that even the birth of a new family member was overshadowed.

Death is the only phenomenon that brings science and religion into a sort of unholy and unscientific matrimony to discuss any possible way out. It is also the fear of the unknown and raises questions about what comes after this life. Even those who do not believe in consciousness after this life are often fearful about their own death. I have heard a great variety of answers regarding this very issue. Some believe that after this life we will turn into something else, such as a tree or an animal, and some believe we will turn into energy. But these conjectures still do not take away our fear.

Life After Life: In 1975, Dr. Raymond Moody's best-selling book entitled Life After Life focused public attention on near-death experience like never before. It was Moody who actually coined the term "near-death experience" (NDE). Moody is also the author of The Light Beyond, Reunions, Life After Loss, Coming Back, Reflections, and The Last Laugh. He did not practice any religion. The psychologist and philosopher who grew up as the son of an agnostic surgeon was simply curious about the phenomenon of what happens when we die.

Since then, thousands of experiences of those who have died (or who almost died but recovered) have been recorded and compared. Moody's research covers decades of inquiry into the NDE phenomenon. He spent 50 years studying the issue alone. He outlines nine elements that generally occur during NDEs. After 50 years of work, he says he has "woken up to God."

Love and Care: Over 30 million people from different backgrounds and cultures have reported an NDE. In the USA alone, eight million people have technically died but returned back to life. More than 60 percent have described similar experiences. Are they lying? How can that be possible if they include many different cultures, ethnicities, creeds, and races?

Just to be clear, one is medically pronounced dead when his/her heart stops and there is no breath detected—even with life support, they would be considered "brain dead." The following nine experiences were the most common among reported NOE experiences.

1. *A strange sound:* A buzzing or ringing noise, while still having a sense of being dead.

2. *Peace and painlessness:* While people are dying, they may be in intense pain. As soon as they leave the body, the pain vanishes, and they experience peace.

3. *Out-of-body experience:* The dying often have a sensation of rising up and floating above their own body while it is surrounded by a medical team. They watch it down below, feeling comfortable. They experience the feeling of being in a spiritual body that appears to be a sort of living energy field. (When they come back to life, they explain what was happening while they were considered to be dead.)

4. *The tunnel experience:* The next experience is that of being drawn into darkness through a tunnel, at an extremely high speed, until reaching a realm of radiant golden-white light. They sometimes report feeling scared, but they do not sense that they were on the way to hell or that they fell into it. (Light is indeed a very spiritual element that seems to communicate the message of love, compassion, and care to the individual.)

5. *Rising rapidly into the heavens:* Instead of a tunnel, some people report rising suddenly into the heavens and seeing the earth and celestial sphere, as it would be seen by astronauts in space.

6. *People of light:* Once on the other side of the tunnel, or after they have risen into the heavens, the dying meet people who glow with an inner light. They find that friends and relatives who have already died are there to greet them.

7. *The Being of Light:* After meeting the people of light, the dying often meet a powerful spiritual being, who some have identified as God, Jesus, or some other religious figure.

8. *The life review:* The Being of Light presents the dying with a panoramic review of everything they have ever done. That is, they relive every act they have ever done to other people and come away feeling that love is the most important thing in life.

9. *Reluctance to return:* The Being of Light sometimes tells the dying that they must return to life. Other times, they are given a choice of staying or returning. In either case, they are reluctant to return. The people who choose to return generally do so only because of loved ones they do not wish to leave behind.[6]

Please be aware that this is all secular research, yet I find it amusing that people felt a presence of a *spiritual being*. They did not think about anything but love and care. Millions of them did not believe in the love or care of others before, let alone God, but, after these near death experiences, many of them professed a new faith in love and relationships and a new belief in a higher power. It is fascinating how these millions of people experienced exactly what the Bible teaches.

Endnotes

6   Raymond Moody, Life After Life: The Investigation of a Phenomenon--Survival of Bodily Death (New York: HarperCollins Publishers, 2001).

Chapter 5
The Supremacy of Belief Over Rationale

Some people choose to believe in eternity. Others choose to deny the very existence of eternity. We are here now, that is physical evidence of the existence of the present. No one has seen all of eternity; therefore, it is hard to believe in such a thing. I am not going to give you all of the answers you are looking for here in this book, but I do want to point out a constant struggle that I see in our world. There are those who would like to live forever in this world, and then there are those who would rather not. Let us suppose that my choices are going to determine my personal perception of eternity. The question I should be asking then, is not whether there is such a thing as eternity or not. We should closely consider the fact that, if there is eternity, then it exists whether or not we believe in it, therefore, my choices merely affect my own quality of 'life' (be it suffering or bliss) in eternity.

Belief: When one says "I believe in the choices that we make, and I choose not to believe in eternity," what is that person really saying? Our choices are subject to our beliefs, not the other way around. One may argue that we can believe in whatever we want and make choices to do whatever we want, but no one will argue that there is a definite connection between our choices and our ability to believe. Furthermore, though we do have the freedom to choose what we believe in, we do not have the power for those choices to actually affect the ultimate truth of what is reality and what is not.

If a man tells me that he can cross Niagara Falls from the US side to the Canadian side by walking on a rope tied onto both ends, it is my choice to believe him or not. I may object and be a cynic until he actually shows me that he can do so in pictures, or perhaps in a video. At this point, it becomes my choice to believe him or to require further evidence to prove that the pictures and videos are legitimate. In that case, he may go ahead and walk across the falls right before my eyes, and if the man then said, "Do you believe now?" I would have to say yes because I saw him do so with my own eyes. Belief is something that we feel deep down in our guts and in our soul. Based on his performance, if he now says, "I believe that I am so good at this, that I could put my son on my shoulders and cross the falls with him," I may say, "Is it really worth it to jeopardize your son's life just to prove your point?" However, his question was not about whether or not he should do this, but whether or not I believed in his skills enough to say that he could do it. If he then successfully crossed the falls while carrying his son on his shoulders just to prove his point, I would then undoubtedly have to believe in his ability beyond a shadow of a doubt. What would then happen if he asks me, do I believe enough in his skills to jump on his shoulder while he crosses? Can I do it?

Our choices and beliefs are interconnected, but when it is a matter of life and death, most of us try to abstain from making choices that can hurt us. Despite this, when we passionately believe in a cause, most of us are willing to make the hard choices regardless of potentially negative consequences. We choose to fight harder for a cause because we believe in it, not because of any rational thought.

Cause: It is very hard for a skeptic mind to understand why one can give his or her own life for a cause. It seems a bit irrational to sacrifice something or everything for a single belief, yet, from the beginning of mankind, we see a pattern of believing in a cause and sacrificial choices being made for that belief. This is how the nations were established and defended, inventions and discoveries were made, and much knowledge was brought to light for the benefit of generations to come. Is a cause worth fighting for when we know that the price we pay is shockingly little compared to the joy we receive at the end?

Joy: This simple three letter word has so much power in it. All of us know someone in our life who always seems to be happy, always smiling and joyful. A joyful heart can turn a simple, ugly landscape into a blooming garden worthy of a poem. Joy can overlook the ugliness and unfairness of this world. If we have the choice to be happy and joyful for the rest of our lives, will we not work for it? We work to build beautiful mansions for ourselves, we earn as much as we can, we seek love in human beings, and we do everything we can to find a kind of joy that can last forever. If I eat a delicious meal or watch a wonderful movie, it may give me temporary joy, but in the long run I will be back in the streets searching for a permanent fix. Does this mean that we are meant to be unsatisfied?

Existence, "meant to be": When anyone uses the phrase "meant to be," the person assumes predestination. Usually, the term is used for cosmological events and human life. It points towards the supernatural and is an idea that is so intriguing that, for centuries, scholars, philosophers, and theologians have spent limitless hours arguing and debating the subject. This is simply because predestination assumes that there is someone who has preplanned the set course of our actions in life. In other words, there was once a time when we and this universe never existed, but then both came into existence through a supernatural power and will cease to exist if the supernatural decides to make everything go away. What should we do if this is true, and if the one who created us brings an end to our lives?

Conclusion: No matter how you look at life, death, the universe, and us, people from all walks of life have wondered throughout history and come to one conclusion- there is a higher authority that is above and beyond our reach. It has been called the unknown, the all-powerful, and many other names, yet we all somehow believe in the existence of such a being He is the cause behind things that happened in this world. The end result is always the same: though human rationality ends, the desperate need to find out more never does. Our search for the divine begins when we seek answers or hope to find an object to blame for everything that is beyond our understanding and control. This is where one's beliefs kick in. This all begins with belief and ends with belief. This proves the supremacy of belief over rationality. "All doubts, however skeptical and cynical they may seem, are really a set of alternate beliefs."[7]

Endnotes

7   Timothy Keller, The Reason for God: Belief in an Age of Skepticism, (New York: Dutton, 2008), xvii.

Part Two
Rethinking God

Chapter 6
The Existence of God

Today we are surrounded by many intellectual struggles. Atheism, Deism, Existentialism, Humanism, Darwinism, Evolutionism, etc. I call them intellectual struggles because they involve reasoning, doubts, and beliefs, and they struggle to maintain their existence against each other. Atheism says that there is no God, period. Deists believe there is a supreme being, a "god" who created everything and then left it alone. Basically, Deists believe that there is no interference of a supernatural being in human life. Existentialism assumes that people are entirely free and thus responsible for what they make of themselves. We do not have time here to go through them all, but the point is this-no worldview of previous movements have dared to threaten our society. They were merely an attempt to look at the world and interpret life accordingly.

Postmodernism: In this era of Postmodernism, where everything is supposedly relative, "tolerance" is the new excuse for rejecting right and wrong. The misleading definition of tolerance is confusing our generation, especially our youth. American ethics and moral values that once were very dear to us are losing their meanings and, perhaps intentionally, being redefined. There is a clear sense among religious people that every effort to reduce the influence of religion and God in our society has been meant to marginalize the religious institutions. People of faith believe that the misconception is this: if we can get rid of God, we can get rid of religions, and consequently, division, hate, and terrorism, and achieve global peace. According to the atheists' view, the problem is that, when you throw God out of the picture, what you have left is a huge mess of self-centeredness and self-righteousness.

Therefore, a case can be made on behalf of those who believe in God: that the deepest level of our crises is not the ever changing cultural, religious, or intellectual problems, but the spiritual ones. Spiritual problems require spiritual solutions. In the absence of an absolute truth, there is no realistic scale to measure what is right and what is wrong. But postmodernists believe that there is not such a thing as an absolute truth. A postmodernist does not view the outside word as error; rather other people's truths are true to them and should not be widely rejected. Therefore, the argument postmodernists raise is that no one has the authority to define general truth or impose their own truth upon others. They believe that truth is relative, and truth is up to each individual to determine for him or herself.

Secularism: Herein lies another general misunderstanding based on the analysis of historical and anthropological data about the West (and about most of the world): that is slowly but surely killing our values, morals and the very social fabric of this world is not the decline of religion spirituality, but the rise of secularism. It is the secularist idea that we are much better off now than ever before. Are we? Is it not true that the world is becoming a worse place every day, with more crime, more illnesses, and more disease? Yes, we may have progressed in science and technology, but we definitely have regressed in our ethical and moral values. In short, the allegation against secularists is that secularism promotes a cheap substitute to confrontation, reasoning, and fighting for the cause that one believes in. If everyone's truth is real truth, why do we have so much hatred, terrorism, and war? Injustice's triumph cannot be more glorious than it is in a gloomy, morally corrupt world, that is somehow perceived as civilized and high standard.

Four Arguments About The Existence of God

There are many arguments about the existence of God based solely on history, science, personal experiences, and philosophy. However, there are four primary philosophical arguments about the existence of God that are respected by intellectuals. These four arguments can be listed as:

1. *The ontological argument:* This argument invites a thinker to examine God, noting that, in order to deny His existence one must understand the idea of Him. If this is so, then God must exist at least as an idea in the mind of the very person who is attempting to deny Him. What is the idea of God? To Anselm (to whom this argument is credited), God is the greatest possible being. He writes, "... we believe that thou art a being than which none greater can be conceived."[8] C. Stephen Evans, in his book Philosophy of Religion, put the argument into numbered steps: 1) God is the greatest possible being; 2) God exists at least in the mind or understanding; 3) a being that exists only in the mind is not so great as a being who exists in reality as well as in the mind; 4) if God exists only in mind then, he would not be the greatest possible being; 5) hence, God must exist in reality as well as in the mind.[9]

2. *The first cause argument:* There is a list of such arguments, but they all come under the umbrella of the cosmological arguments. This states that the universe came into existence at a point in the distant past. Since nothing can

come into existence unless there is something to bring it into existence, there must be some being outside of the universe that caused the universe to exist. In short, God must exist as the first or ultimate cause of the universe.

3. *The teleological argument:* Also referred to as "the argument from design," this argument falls under a cosmological argument as well. In a nut shell, the universe could have been different in many ways from the one we have. It could have had different laws of physics; it could have had a different arrangement of planets and stars, etc. Although the majority of these many forms are possible, they would not have allowed for the existence of life. The sscientific and atheistic world views have no way to explain this good fortune; therefore, they must put it down to chance. However, the possibility of a higher being or power (God) explains why the universe is the way that it is: God created the universe for the existence of life (humans), yet that life (humans) questions His existence.

4. *The moral argument:* This argument is based on moral law, and the question it raises is this: "Is there evil in this world?" Beyond a shadow of a doubt, the answer is "yes." If there is evil in this world, you cannot deny that there is good as well. We all know what we ought to do regardless of whether we do so or not. This is due to the moral law that has always existed in this world. Place to place, it might have had less or more influence, but every human society has always practiced this law in some shape or form. So, if there is moral law in this world, then there must be a moral lawgiver, and that moral lawgiver is God. As the first cause argument states, there is always

a first cause, and in this case God is the first cause. "Like the teleological argument, the moral argument is best construed probabilistically, as a claim that God's existence provides the most probable or plausible explanation of a certain fact, in this case the existence of moral obligation. The reasoning is this: 1) (Probably) unless there is a God, there cannot be objectively morally binding obligations; 2) There are objectively binding moral obligations; 3) Therefore (probably) there is a God."[10]

Endnotes

8   Princeton University, "Anselm's Ontological Argument." http://www.princeton. edu/~grosen/puc/phi203/ontological.html (accessed June 23, 2014).

9   C. Stephen Evans, Philosophy of Religion. (Downers Grove: InterVarsity Press, 1982), 69.

10 Ibid.

Chapter 7
The Idea of Rethinking God

In 1882, Friedrich Nietzsche refuted the theological explanation of things that have no rational understanding by insisting that "God is dead. God remains dead. And we have killed him."[11] The idea of God has always been a part of human history. In ancient times, people relied on God more than in modern times. The advocates of secularism have been combining their forces to get rid of God, yet, the more they try, the more they make God a central figure, thus inviting masses to begin their own reasoning about God. There seems to be a "God-shaped hole" in the human heart. This hole is a terrifying bottomless abyss opening up inside of us, a hole we would do anything to fill, even denying the very existence of God. John Micklethwaith and Adrian Wooldridge in their book, *God is Back: How the global revival of faith is changing the world* write:

> *One solution to the loss of faith was to find an alternative in secular ideology. These ideologies were at once substitutes and antidotes: substitutes because they helped to satisfy the yearning for meaning; antidotes because for the most part they tried to marginalize religion still further. Four secular faiths sprung to the fore in the nineteenth century: science, culture, the nation-state and socialism.*[12]

God: Some would say, "If everything is meant to be, then let it happen. I will continue to do whatever I am doing, whether it is evil or good, because the Creator is the one who sets the course of my life, and He has already predestined every choice that I make." However, given the evidence that I am not a robot, and I have the will and the power to do almost everything that a human being is expected to do, I should then be more concerned about my life in eternity because, if God is all powerful, all knowing, and all-controlling, then I should aim to do that which may please him. If He decides to be worshiped, He can use His power to make us worship Him. Yet it is the very nature of God that, in His creative design, He left a gap to be filled with God and the freedom to decide as how we might fill that "God-Shaped hole." "Religious choice has a profound effect on public life. The more that people choose their religion— rather than just inherit it—the more likely they are to make a noise about it."[13] Subsequently, crime rates will go down, and moral and ethical values will rise. This is not something that advocates of religion came up with, but the reflection of data from communities where the crime rate went down as a direct result of religious influence. In New York City, many of those neighborhoods that were once considered high crime areas have been transformed into peaceful neighborhoods because of a religious presence. According to Prison Fellowship International, no other program in U.S. correctional facilities has as resounding positive outcomes as faith-based organizations like PFI because they address the deeper issues relating to the soul rather than trying to change people psychologically.

Free Will: The idea of free will is very deep and crucial to the character of God. It is something He revealed to us so that we may appreciate not only His character but also His heart.

One can sub-categorize the reasons behind the blessing of Free Will in three ways:

1. *Relationship:* More than anything, God desires glorification, and a type of glorification that only He can provide. Glorification is possible by humans only through a true relationship, where both parties mutually agree to be committed to each other. Like any other healthy relationship, the involved individuals become one without losing their individuality. Love, respect and care are three out of many willful characteristics or attributes manifested in a healthy relationship. It is not out of any obligation or completion that one shows love, care, and respect; rather, it is an unspoken, willful act.

2. *Love:* In order to initiate such a relationship, God granted us free will so that we might attempt to love Him as He loves us (although theoretically it is impossible to comprehend God's love), with the intention and desire to develop a healthy and everlasting relationship. It is twofold:

   a. Free will is a manifestation of God's unconditional love, where He alone proposes that we develop a relationship based on our personal decisions and commitment.

   b. Not only does He love, but He is love. And if He is the embodiment of love, then how can He do something that absolutely contradicts Himself? How could He receive a robotic or forced love, an illusion questioning His integrity and truthfulness?

3. *Justice:* Because God is just, He must let a man make his own choices. By nature, He seeks justice, and it would be unjust to create a being that is loved by God but is incapable of free will.

This raises some of the most common ethical and moral questions. For me, if we are His creation, then we should please Him. But how can a mere human being please an almighty God? If He is creator, designer, master and father, He must desire that His creation obey Him, but Why would he have created us with free will if He desires us to obey Him? It is imperative to decide now where we will search for such crucial and fundamental questions about God.

Search: It is a desire and passion to find. You may have a desire, but, if you do not have a passion for the search, you may quit and end up never finding what you were looking for. Most of the time, humans tend to look in the wrong places, and other times we do not even know what we are looking for. There is a desire in us to search—perhaps for love, wealth, fame, or relationships—but many of us do so simply because those are the things that most people over the years have desired and searched for. It is easy to do what has already been done and to follow what is defined according to the world's social standards. Ralph Waldo Emerson a 19th century American scholar, said once, "Do not go where the path may lead; go instead where there is no path, and leave a trail." Sometimes the danger in following a path taken by others lies in the fact that you may never know what you have missed on the road less traveled. Likewise, social standards give us an inside peek at adult life, even before we are able to understand the full meaning of being "grown up." So whatever we hear, see and observe around us, our nature encourages us to adopt it. Needs and wants then lose their differences.

What if the world and the very people around you were mistaken about what they were searching for? In many parts of the world, especially in Asia, children go to school and study for a major that their parents essentially decide for them. Here in

America and the West, the tradition was similar until the dawn of the twentieth century when children were encouraged to do what they wanted and to study any subject. The worst case of ignorance exists not when you lack knowledge or access to it, but when you are aware that the knowledge is out there, and yet you remain ignorant of the fact that you are missing out.

Endnotes

11 Friedrich Nietzsche, The Gay Science (1882, 1887) para. 125; Walter Kaufmann ed. (New York: Vintage, 1974), pp.181-82.

12 John Micklethwaith and Adrian Wooldridge, God is Back: How the global revival of faith is changing the world (New York: The Penguin Press, 2009), 44.

13 Ibid.,24.

Chapter 8
The Polarization of Our Being

No one likes to admit that they are wrong. Some of us are so stubborn that we would rather lose everything than simply acknowledge our faults. Our pursuit of freedom and happiness leads us to all kinds of conclusions; even when we are wrong we want to defend our brand of happiness. Culture encourages such a mindset. It has produced polarization in our society and within us. What is considered a crime to one is freedom of expression to another; and what is disgusting to one is desirable to another. Perhaps, then, we do not find ultimate happiness because we are looking in the wrong place with the wrong motives and without a unified expression of happiness. One may think that he is making himself happy when he heinously molests a child or rapes a woman, even though both are serious criminal actions in the United States, but these same actions have no legal ramification in many cultures where young girls are given away to be married as children and where women aren't given any kind of legal rights for the protection of their bodies. Therefore, it can be argued that individual and cultural ideas regarding happiness are subjective to one's opinion.

John Micklethwaith and Adrian Wooldridge quoting Michael Burleigh from his book *Earthly Power* wrote, "Culture wasn't just a substitute for religion but was superior to it. Culture wasn't contaminated with barbarism or superstition. Culture didn't generate wars or persecution. Culture-and particularly music-provided the distilled essence of religion free from the stains of dogmatism and warfare."[14] The cult of culture that flourished in the nineteenth century noticeably became a substitute for religion in the West. This was largely an attempt to civilize and redeem mankind from perceived superstitions, and it polarized society faster than any religion could have done in several centuries time. Matthew Arnold writes, "Culture, disinterestedly seeking in its aim at perfection to see things they really are, shows us how worthy and divine a thing is the religious side in man, though it is not the whole man."[15]

Another problem is a lack of focus and prioritization in our life and in the important choices that we make; these determine how devoted we are and provide us with a systematic approach to accomplish our goals. We should be more than just "me, my and I." Bigger than us as individuals is the purpose of our life and our being; our individual being is just another small particle living on a slightly larger particle of dust floating in the unimaginably vast universe. We all fall into two categories: that of a narrow focus or that of a broad focus. Narrow-focused people can be narrow minded; broad-focused people can endanger their searches by being too open minded. All of us are narrow minded to a certain degree, even if we appear to be open minded. We discover boundaries within our open mindedness when we reflect on our personal encounters, likes and dislikes. Can these ways of thinking (broad and narrow) usher us into success? Another aspect of happiness is the search for success, the measurement of which is another highly subjective matter.

Success: We measure success the same way we measure priorities. We look at our immediate physical needs and prioritize our life, time, and energy around them. Success often seems attainable when we measure our path by worldly standards. Let us not forget that, generally speaking, the richer you become, the more unhappy and dissatisfied you are. When there is nothing left to achieve or conquer in life, how can one find anything meaningful? The third king of Israel, Solomon, who was and still is famous for his wisdom, wrote a piece of wisdom; it is a bit philosophical, but it shows us the states of worldly success:

> *I, the Teacher, was king over Israel in Jerusalem. I applied my mind to study and to explore by wisdom all that is done under the heavens. What a heavy burden God has laid on mankind! I have seen all the things that are done under the sun; all of them are meaningless, a chasing after the wind.*
>
> *What is crooked cannot be straightened; what is lacking cannot be counted.*
>
> *I said to myself, "Look, I have increased in wisdom more than anyone who has ruled over Jerusalem before me; I have experienced much of wisdom and knowledge." Then I applied myself to the understanding of wisdom, and also of madness and folly, but I learned that this, too, is a chasing after the wind.*
>
> *For with much wisdom comes much sorrow; the more knowledge, the more grief.*[16]

Meaningless: Scientifically, as humans, our perception of the meta-physical world leads us to makes assumptions. Assumptions propose a thesis or statement of a problem, then research is launched to validate whether the assumption is correct or incorrect. When experiments are done and results are retrieved, we use the data to predict the cause behind a problem. If we find a solution to the problem by resolving the cause of it, we say that our research contributed to the science or art at hand. Even though we arrived at the solution due to existing problems, it is still considered to be a contribution because a new direction is now available to do further research.

It seems perfectly acceptable to make assumptions in a scientific matter, but when it comes to life we cannot live like an experiment. We learn from our mistakes and strive to find ways to make our lives worth living for. A meaningless life is worse than death. Assume whatever you do is meaningless because nothing is permanent. If nothing is permanent, then perhaps the thesis or the problem should subsequently be meaningless.

Permanent: In this world, nothing will last forever, not even the stars. It has been scientifically proven that many stars much bigger than our sun have eventually died off. That is the fate of our sun, too. Our natural resources, such as water, share the same fate. It is noted recently that, "The Arctic has been undergoing significant changes in recent years. Surface temperatures in the region are rising twice as fast as the global mean. The extent and thickness of sea ice is rapidly declining. Such changes may have an impact on atmospheric conditions outside the region."[17] Another search reports states, "The Arctic is now front and center in the midst of many impotent questions facing the world today. Our daily weather, what we eat, and coastal flooding and all interconnected with the future of the Arctic."[18] We are running out of resources, and we are expecting and experiencing more natural disasters in the present day, yet there is nothing that we can do to stop it. We are helpless before the cruelty of nature. If we run out of resources we will not be able to sustain life on this planet. The destruction of the earth and the world is, then, imminent. Now we can make an intelligent case for the creationists: If there is a God, and He created everything why would He not make the world indestructible?

"If" Issue with God: There is a long list of "if" issues with God. Every issue follows science to answer critical questions about the nature of God. It seems ironic that, even though one does not believe in God or religion, when a natural disaster hits, God is blamed right away. How can one blame something on someone who they refuse to acknowledge the existence of? All the "if" questions regarding God have three things in common: 1) an unbelieving heart; 2) a skeptic nature; and 3) anger and pride—all geared towards God. No one has been able to determine what are the right questions are to be asking regarding God. If one believes that God is a divine, real being who is transcendent and has willfully exposed Himself to us, then we must seek the proper outlet for His self-exposure. However one does not believe should investigate his or her own reasoning behind such skepticism. Is it personal or scientific? Either way investigating the truth of God should be given at least the same unbiased attention, time and energy that are given to discover other scientific truths. Nevertheless, if God is the eternal and everything else is temporary then our brilliance became our failure and the end our life would have no meanings.

Endnotes

14 Micklethwaith and Wooldridge God is Back: How the global revival of faith is changing the world.45 quoted Michael Burleigh, Earthly Powers: 272-3.

15 Matthew Arnold, Culture and Anarchy (New York: AMS Press, 1970), XLI.

16 The Book of Ecclesiastes 1:12-18, New International Version.

17 National Research Council. Linkages Between Arctic Warming and Mid-Latitude Weather Patterns: Summary of a Workshop (Washington, DC: The National Academies Press, 2014),1.

18 National Research Council. The Arctic in the Anthropocene: Emerging Research Questions (Washington, DC: The National Academies Press, 2014), 11.

Chapter 9
The Problem of Pain and God

On top of natural disasters, we experience pain everyday in our own lives. There is hunger, injustice, hate, anger, illness, abuse, broken relationships, betrayal, sorrow, disappointment, injuries, heartaches, crime and death. Whether you believe in God or not, it is very human to shout, "Why? Why me? Why now? Why did this happen to me? What did I do to deserve this?" "Such questions may be raised in anger or laced with self-pity or even murmured in depression. But every such question is the heart's protest against the disruption and disorder in evil and suffering."[19] In his hour of pain Thomas Carlyle said "There is no religion; there is no God; man has lost his soul, and vainly seeks antiseptic salt."[20] When we are going through pain, we either cling to God for help, or we reject God for not helping us instantly. The interesting element in this process is again the fact that, even though we claim that there is no God, somehow we blame Him for our travesties and grievances.

In C. S Lewis words:

> Our present condition, then, is explained by the fact
> that we are members of a spoiled species. I do not
> mean that our sufferings are a punishment for being
> what we cannot now help being nor that we are morally
> responsible for the rebellion of a remote ancestor. If,
> none the less I can our present condition one of orig-

inal Sin, and not merely one of original misfortune,
that is because our actual religious experience does
not allow us to regard it in any way.[21]

It seems that religion should have the answer to the problem of pain; however, many religious people struggle with an unprecedented amount of pain in their own lives. Some come to believe that it is the will of God for them to struggle so, while others continue to struggle without arriving at a definite answer. Others make a quick exit, leaving their religion to try another, or quitting the idea of faith all together.

"Why": Unanswered questions lead to more questions. "Why" is by far the most tormenting question in the entire history of humankind. Early in my life, I learned three ways to deal with many of the "Why?" questions. At times, when my home back in Pakistan was constantly under attack because of our faith, when my dad was in jail for his faith, when my mother was in pain and doctors could not tell us why, as a young boy I always wondered, "Why?" "Why my mom?" She was the most faithful and godly person I had ever met. Here are the three things I learned: 1) when you cannot trace God's hand, you can trust His heart; 2) faith that cannot be tested cannot be trusted; and 3) a reason for living is an excellent reason for dying. Unlike me, my mother didn't ask the "why" questions because she believed that *Death is imminent and upon each and every one of us. No one can escape it; therefore, we should live our lives so that, when we die, we might have no regrets.* Thus, she continues to live an exemplary life of faith, patience, perseverance, and humility.

There is no escape from death; even the availability of the best medicine can buy us only a few extra days, months or maybe even a couple of years, only to give in to the brutal reality of death in the end. We place our lives in the hands of medical doctors, believing that science, technology, and medicine will redeem us from our pain. The most brilliant doctors of medicine are no more than human; they are full of human error, just as any of us. The only difference is that they chose medicine as their profession and calling in life. In our professions we may have the second, third, or fourth chance to fix our mistakes, but they often do not have such a luxury. More people die in a given year as a result of medical errors than from motor vehicle accidents (43, 458), breast cancer (42,297), or AIDS (16,516).[22] Even when using the lower estimate, deaths due to medical errors exceed the number attributable to the 8th-leading cause of death.[23] "These figures offer only a very modest estimate of the magnitude of the problem since hospital patients represent only a small proportion of the total population at risk."[24] This does not mean that we should not consult doctors when we are ill; it is simply to show that there is a bigger power who is errorless in contrast to anything that man can offer, including science and the most sophisticated technology that we lean on. Where we should go with our problems? To a man like us, or to someone who is above and beyond us? The resentment that keeps us from accepting God as the only source of our comfort has encouraged many exceptional thinkers of our time to invent and present a new reason to hate and reject God. John Micklethwait and Adrian Wooldridge, commenting on the faith of religious people, write:

> *Freud compared the obsessive behavior of reli-gious people-repeating prayers, performing rituals and so on-to the obsessive behavior of neurotics. He insisted that the belief in God was just another manifestation of the "father complex": religious people cling to the idea of God because they haven't managed to escape from their infantile belief in the almighty father. To be religious is to be trapped in*

childhood-taking comfort in an illusory protector and refusing to grow up. And, as if being childish is not bad enough, religious people are also female children: they want to be possessed by a masculine god. (Many of Freud's most religious male patients fantasized about changing their sex.) He argued that losing faith in religion is part of growing up: once we realize that our parents are not all-mighty and all knowing, once we come to terms with our human limitations, we lose our belief in God.[25]

Contrary to what Freud suggested, religion says, if humans accept their limitations, it will bring them to their knees, and they have a moment of self-examination that can lead to God. As undesirable as it is, pain opens doors for us to surrender our self-efforts and human pride to God, and, consequently, when we are fully exhausted with our own efforts, we seek God. If you have not yet asked why our world is infected with pain and suffering, and why God allows these things, I guarantee you will once you or a loved one is stricken with full force. Everyone raises "Why?" questions sooner or later, even Jesus on the cross in His humanity. According to Scripture, He raised a question to His Father (God): "Why have you forsaken me?" (Matthew 27:46 ESV).

Unlike some other religious leaders who wrote off pain and suffering as mere illusions, Jesus was honest about the inevitability of suffering. In John 16:33 he said, "You shall have suffering in this world."[26] He did not say you might—He said it is going to happen. He suffered himself. In Matthew 10:24, He proclaimed, "A disciple is not above his teacher, nor a servant above his master" (ESV).

In recent years, our world has been stricken by more death, hunger, homelessness, pain, and natural disaster than ever before. Some of these incidents were so painful that there are no adequate words to express the anguish experienced. Many people are asking the question, "Why? Why did God allow this?" When we experience our own personal pain, we are far more likely to raise questions about God than when we observe the pain of others. When it is about you or someone you love, then you ask 'why me?' Distance is key when it comes to pain and suffering. The further away the pain of an individual, group, or nation is, the less we feel its stinging effect.

In his book, *Unspeakable Facing up to the Challenge of Evil*, Os Guinness writes:

> *The final pressure in the question "Why me" comes from the dull obvious fact that for the rest of the world life just goes on. That is not how we feel it should be. What does hit us is like a hurt that throbs and throbs and allows us to think of nothing else. Just as we smash a hammer on a thumb and become all thumb, or stub a toe and become all toe, so the hurts in our lives shout for attention—and the bigger the hurt, the more it screams to be center of the universe. We are hurting, and it is so painful that everyone should care. Anyone who does not surely has a deficiency of humanity.[27]*

Arguments against God: The argument about suffering is that, if God is all good and all powerful, then why does He allow suffering in this world? Therefore, either He is not all powerful, as Christians believe (otherwise He would have stopped it), or He is not all good (otherwise He wouldn't sit back and let suffering exist in the world He created. These questions are framed in a way that supplies the questioner with the answer he wants to retrieve. Spiritually and biblically speaking, it presupposes that the sin of mankind should go unpunished, that no one should be held responsible for his or her actions. This does not mean that all the suffering and sickness in the world is a result of sins that we may have committed, but certainly the root of all suffering and pain sprouted out of the sin of Adam. It can be traced very easily back to the fall of Adam. Here, I want to make two points:

1. Although the source of all pain and suffering is always sin, it is certainly not always God.

2. Although God is always able to deliver us from pain and suffering whether it is from His hand or not, He always acts according to His good and perfect will, and sometimes this means inaction.

Endnotes

19 Guinness, Unspeakable: Facing up to the challenge of evil, 52.

20 Quoted in A. N. Wilson, God's Funeral (New York: Norton, 1999), 69.

21 C.S. Lewis, The problem of Pain (New York: HarperCollins Publishers, 1996), 81

22 Centers for Disease Control and Prevention (National Center for Health Statistics). "Births and Deaths: Preliminary Data for 1998," National Vital Statistics Reports. 47(25): 1999: 6.

23 American Hospital Association. Hospital Statistics. Chicago. 1999. See also: Brennan, Troyen A.; Leape, Lucian L.; Laird, Nan M., et al. Incidence of adverse events and negligence in hospitalized patients: Results of the Harvard Medical Practice Study I. N Engl J Med. 324:370–376, 1991. See also: Leape, Lucian L.; Brennan, Troyen A.; Laird, Nan M., et al. The Nature of Adverse Events in Hospitalized Patients: Results of the Harvard Medical Practice Study II. N Engl J Med. 324(6):377–384, 1991.

24 Institute of Medicine. To Err Is Human: Building a Safer Health System. (Washington, DC: The National Academies Press, 2000), 2

25 Micklethwaith et al., God is Back: How the global revival of faith is changing the world, 42-43.

26 Aramaic Bible in Plain English

27 Ibid., 56.

Chapter 10
The Simple Answer to Complicated Questions

God is loving and all powerful. He can do whatever He wants. There is no one in the known or unknown world who can challenge His authority. Daniel 4:35, says "All the peoples of the earth are regarded as nothing. He does as He pleases with the powers of heaven and the peoples of the earth. No one can hold back his hand or say to him: 'What have you done?'" (NIV). "He is before all things, and in him all things hold together" Col. 1:17 (NIV).

Spiritual Compass: In His own divine wisdom, God decided to give us the freedom to make our own choices, to choose between good and evil, right and wrong. Although He clearly provided us with a spiritual compass to navigate our moral and spiritual decisions, human choices in their totality are ours. Without free will, man is no more than a robot. You may say, "Well, that would have been good, because then I would not have offended God not gotten into any trouble." This, however, would defeat God's purpose of creating human beings; robotic creatures are not capable of the intimate relationship that God desires from us. Love is a voluntary act, and if you force someone to love you, then it is really not love.

Why Us?: This raises an excellent question about why God created us to begin with. The Psalmist writes, "When I consider your heavens, the work of your fingers ... what is man that you are mindful of him, and the son of man that you care for him?" (Psalm 8:3-4 ESV). Dawson McAllister determined three answers to the question, "Why did God make us?"

1. *It was not because God needed us*. The God who made the world and everything in it ... is not served by human hands, as if he needed anything (Acts 7:24-25). And He did not make us because he was lonely. Long before we were here, God already had "company" with His Son and the Holy Spirit, referred to in Genesis 1:26, "Let us make man in our own image."

   And he did not make us because He needed His ego fed. It is not as if God made us just to satisfy a craving to be worshiped. God is totally secure in who He is—without us.

2. *Despite not needing us, God chose to create us anyway, out of His great love*. "I have loved you with an ever-lasting love" (Jeremiah 31:3). Yes, God loved us before He even created us. It is impossible to get our heads around that idea, but it is true; that is what "everlasting" love means.

   God is love (1 John 4:8), and because of that love and His wonderful creativity, He made us so that we can enjoy all that He is and all that He's done.

3. *God created us to fulfill His eternal plan*. God, in His infinite wisdom, chose to make us a part of His eternal plan. Perhaps the most important part we can play in God's eternal plan is to point other people to eternal life with God—through His Son, Jesus Christ. The Bible calls this our "ministry of reconciliation" (2 Corinthians 5:18-19).

That is why we are here. But it is also important to note that we have a choice in all of this. When God created us, He did not make us pawns in some cosmic chess game. We are not His toy soldiers. God gives us freedom of choice.

The bottom line is this: He lets us make our own choices. God may not need us, but we certainly need Him. Whether we make good or bad choices is entirely on us.

Evil: There is another complicated question that is raised against those who believe in God and who believe that God has created everything. Who created evil? The premise is that, if God created everything, then everything includes evil. There are many books written on this subject, but here is a simple answer: just as the absence of light is dark or darkness, similarly the absence of God or good is evil. When there is no God, there is evil. God created everything, and He said that it is good. So, God did not create evil—He did not have to; it exists only if and when one rejects God. We make the choice of letting evil take over when we do not have God in us and in the midst of us.

Just as dark is not a "thing," neither is evil. Even though the effects of evil are real, it in itself is not. What we experience on a day to day basis is the effect of such evil carried by us; the true vessels of evil, which inflect pain on ourselves and others. For example, holes are real, but they only exist in something else. We call the absence of dirt a hole, but it cannot be separated from the dirt."[28]

Suffering: It draws us near to God and away from God. I am certainly no authority on how to deal with suffering, but I assure you that I am no stranger to it. According to the Bible the purpose of trials is not to defeat us but to develop our character.

The Bible teaches "Consider it pure joy, my brothers and sisters, whenever you face trials of many kinds, because you know that the testing of your faith produces perseverance. Let perseverance finish its work so that you may be mature and complete, not lacking anything" (James 1:2-4 ESV).

Through trials, God develops our character; we learn the true meaning of perseverance because it is perseverance that makes us mature and lack nothing. Subsequently, when we come out of our trials, we gain a new perspective on life, this world, relationships, and the things around us. This is when we are able to say with the Psalmist, "The Lord is my Shepherd and I shall not want" (Ps. 23:1 KJV).

We learn that we can handle more trials than we initially thought we could. "No trial has overtaken you that is not faced by others. And God is faithful: He will not let you be tried beyond what you are able to bear, but with the trial will also provide a way out so that you may be able to endure it" (1 Corinthians 10:13 NET).

We do not know what the future holds, but we know who holds the future. "Therefore I tell you, do not be anxious about your life, what you will eat or what you will drink, nor about your body, what you will put on. Is not life more than food, and the body more than clothing? Look at the birds of the air: they neither sow nor reap nor gather into barns, and yet your heavenly Father feeds them. Are you not of more value than they? And which of you by being anxious can add a single hour to his span of life? And why are you anxious about clothing?" (Matt. 6:25-34 ESV)

No one has seen our future, not even Satan. God is the only one who is sovereign who knows our future, and He tells us not to worry about it because He has a plan for us. "Do not be anxious about anything, but in everything by prayer and supplication with thanksgiving let your requests be made known to God. And the peace of God, which surpasses all understanding, will guard your hearts and your minds in Christ Jesus" (Philippians 4:6-7 ESV).

No matter how hard it gets, God holds our future and promises us: "He will wipe away every tear from their eyes, and death shall be no more, neither shall there be mourning, nor crying, nor pain anymore, for the former things have passed away" (Rev. 21:4 ESV).

Conclusion: Sometimes suffering is not only good but it is necessary for our life, and health. In November 1937, a nine-year-old American boy who was born without the ability to sense pain was taken to John Hopkins Medical School in Baltimore. We may initially think that not being able to feel pain would be a great; however, this is what the examining doctor wrote in his report:

1. *Partial blindness in one eye because, when he had sand in his eye, he did not notice it until permanent damage had been done.*

2. *Scars on almost every part of his body.*

3. *Enormous scar across his buttocks where he had sat on a heater and did not notice until his flesh was burnt to the bone.*

4. *One foot permanently deformed, as he had broken a bone and walked about on it for months before it was spotted.*

5. *Both hands so badly cut that he would never again be able to straighten his fingers.*

> *We can see that pain acts as a danger signal to the rest*
> *of us, but this unfortunate boy had nothing to warn him*
> *to stop and think when his body was being injured.*[29]

I will present the Christian understanding of why God allows suffering later on by looking at the life of Job.

Endnotes

28 Michael Houdmann, "Did God create evil?," Got Questions?org. http://www.gotquestions.org/did-God-create-evil.html (accessed June 27, 2014).
29 "Life's BIG questions" The Problem of Suffering, http://www.lifes-big-questions.org/Sect3Page2.php. (accessed July 1, 2014).

Part Three
Christ and Christianity

Chapter 11
The Dilemma with Christianity

We must remember that God not only comforts the inflicted, but sometimes inflicts the comfortable. Why does He do this? Perhaps to remind us that He is the boss, or perhaps to let us know not to get too comfortable in this world because it is temporary. Our days on this earth, no matter how long and painful they are, are nothing compared to eternity.

God always has His reasons. God brings us goodness, and He sometimes brings (allows) adversities to test our faith.

When man commits mischief in this world, God is grieved, and when God brings calamity, man is grieved, but the difference is simple. The first is done out of an evil heart to harm, kill and destroy others, and the latter is done out of a pure heart to teach, correct and disciple men. God said, "I form light and create darkness, I make well-being and create calamity, I am the LORD, who does all these things" (Isaiah 45:7 ESV). God is not as much interested in our happiness as He is in our holiness. Being holy means being perfect, and there is no one in this world who is perfect except for God himself. So we always strive to become more holy, and this means striving for perfection everyday in this imperfect world. The more we work at it, the more we become like Him, and the less we define our needs and happiness according to the standards of this world.

False Theology: False theologies of health, wealth and prosperity proclaim that if you are not good with God you will suffer, and if you did something wrong you will suffer. Conversely if you are good with God, then the riches of this world and health will follow you.

1. *God's common grace cares for everyone.* "For He causes His sun to rise on the evil and the good, and sends rain on the righteous and the unrighteous." Matthew 5:45 (NASB)

2. *God is not the God of favoritism.* "Now when Joshua was near Jericho, he looked up and saw a man standing in front of him with a drawn sword in his hand. Joshua went up to him and asked, 'Are you for us or for our enemies?'" "Neither," he replied, . . . Joshua 5:13-14 (NIV)

3. *God patiently awaits our repentance.* "The Lord is not slow concerning His promise, as some regard slowness, but is being patient toward you, because He does not wish for any to perish but for all to come to repentance." 2 Peter 3:9 (NIV)

In everything, God has a purpose. Whether pain and suffering are from the hands of God or not, certainly His hand is able to deliver us. Acts 12 is a beautiful example. It says, "He killed James the brother of John with the sword, and when he saw that it pleased the Jews, he proceeded to arrest Peter also. This was during the days of Unleavened Bread" (Acts 12:2, 3 ESV).

In His sovereign will, God provided a way to escape pain and suffering in this broken world by making Jesus the ransom for all those who come to God though Him. "For Christ also suffered once for sins, the righteous for the unrighteous, that he might bring us to God, being put to death in the flesh but made alive in the spirit" (1 Peter 3:18 ESV). Kassie Logan writes in her poem "The Lady Behind The Walls:"[30]

At times it is a lonely place,
A search for inner happiness,

Yet depression keeps you bound
As I sit and look outside the fence,
At the traffic passing by,
The amazement of it all,
Make me stop and question "Why?"
Why has the Lord bestowed on me,
Such an awesome cross to bear?
Why would the loving God I serve,
Allow something so unfair?
Time to me is nothing new,
Must accept as best I can,
For I know that in the scheme of things,
My Jesus has a plan.
And someday, out those gates I'll walk,
When the Lord's voice gently calls,
And I will tell my story,
About "the lady behind the walls."

Prison of Self: In our own way we are all in a prison, in the prison of this body where we are limited to understand what is beyond our meta-physical world. The prison of rules and regulations; do's and do nots; social norms and cultural barriers, religion and rational; the list goes on and on.

If you take an example of a prisoner, you will find something very unique and profound. People who have spent most of their lives behind bars often admit that they forget how to function out in the world. They become so accustomed to the ways of an inmate life that, even when they come out, they function as if they are still in prison.

In The Shawshank Redemption, Red (Morgan Freeman) states: "These walls are kind of funny. First you hate 'em, then you get used to 'em. Enough time passes, gets so you depend on them. That's institutionalized. They send you here for life, that's exactly what they take. The part that counts, anyways."[31]

I lived twenty five years of my life in a prison that did not have four walls, but had the same effect on me as Red experienced in his movie. As a non-Muslim living in a Muslim state where your rights do not exist as a Christian, you are taught in a systematic way that, even when you are no longer a resident of your own country you will yet struggle to be a free man. Your mind, your being, even your soul becomes institutionalized.

Christianity—Social Suicide: This is the dilemma with Christianity. Unlike other religions, under which you are demanded and institutionalized to follow a certain set of rules and regulations to achieve the highest level of piety, righteousness, and morals, Christianity makes it all about God because man cannot and will not ever be able to reach the level of piety, righteousness, and morals that can satisfy the righteousness and the holiness of God. Therefore, Christianity shares a message about the only time in history when the divine world intersected with the human world. Precisely at that moment, the social, moral, and religious fabric of human society was destroyed, and God was made the only source of understanding, deliverance, and freedom that man thought could help him to achieve peace, prosperity and morality were put to shame.

Unfortunately, today we live in a world where society is trying to choke out our moral values, ethics and God. When we raise the question of right and wrong in this world, we attack the proponents of relativism who believe everything is relative, resulting in social suicide.

Endnotes

30 Bob Schwarz, You Came Unto Me: A Training Manual For Jail And Prison Ministry (Harvest International Network), 16.
31 Russel B. Ramsey, "Shawshank Redmption (Frank Darabont, 1994)," http://www.ransomfellowship.org/articledetail.asp?AID=221&B=Russell%20B.%20Ramsey&TID=2 (accessed June 27, 2014).

Chapter 12
The Misrepresentation
of Christ

Christ, the Church and Christianity all have one thing in common, and that is misrepresentation. The church was to be the reflection of the divine One who condemned the hypocrisy of religious authorities; Christianity was supposed to be the mere image of Christ, whose divine compassion compelled Him to take human form to meet the desperate need for a savior in an ever perishing world; Christ was not to be another deity or super hero to be worshiped and to establish a new religion around him, but to be a total surrender of our beings to the divine man—who was, who is, and who is to come—fully man and fully God. These misrepresentations are not a thing of the recent past or of the modern times only, they have consistently been an issue since the first century.

Church without Christ: In 1928, Dietrich Bonhoeffer noticed that the church had successfully taken Christ out of the community and placed Him within the "temple" of the church, where he was no longer free to make "ridiculous" claims upon people's lives. The church had secularized Christ so that people could further compartmentalize their lives by placing Christ into a specific category of religion. Moreover, Bonhoeffer thought that because Christ had been placed within the boundaries of religion, this allowed people to participate in "temple" without having to take Christ seriously.

In my understanding, this is the byproduct of misrepresentation. Religions in general represent humanity's idea of building a bridge to a God, where men like you and I, with the help of other men (priests, spiritual guides, philosopher and leaders of higher intellect and ethics), attempt to reach the divine. Often, people look mistakenly upon Christ with nothing but admiration for his high standards and his willingness to sacrifice himself, but they refuse to allow Christ to have any sort of definitive claim upon their lives. In Eric Metaxa's biography of Bonhoeffer, he writes, "Christianity was not about a new and better set of behavioral rules or about moral accomplishment."[32] By reducing the divine work of God to a point where humans can contribute and perform moral actions in order to gain access to God (rather than simply placing his or her faith in Christ,) Christianity becomes something that humanity does and claims glory for the self. "Thus, the Christian message is basically amoral and irreligious, paradoxical as that may sound."[33]

Divine Man: God's love for humanity is not enough to save humanity; His justice demands something far greater than what humanity can offer. In its totality, the case of Christ provides the perfect combination of utmost unconditional love and justice,

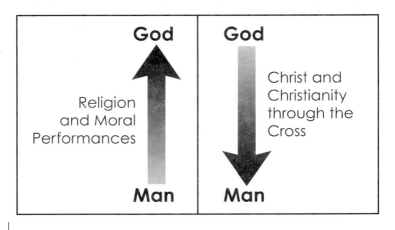

where, at the cross, Christ not only bypassed religion by dying the death of a criminal with no glory whatsoever, but His unblemished life and innocent death for the sake of the world also became an absolute justification for humanity to be reconciled to God.

If religion is the way for man to get to God (which has never yet worked out for humanity), then the cross of Christ is the way for God to get to man (the only way that has ever worked). It is God's love in action: Death on the cross out of His divine love for the sinner becomes the assurance that God's love is with the sinner even through death. The cross is the clear representation of Christ's rejection of worldly power and values.

Satisfaction: Another way to look at the need for the cross is by looking at God. When the Creator decided to become a part of His creation, it was a voluntary, vengeful act to satisfy His wrath against the evil and sin in humanity. Nothing could have contained His divine wrath other than He Himself. No one took His life. Neither the Jews, nor the Romans, nor Satan nor any other power in the world could do that. It was in His will and choice that He gave up His spirit. The death of Christ on the cross was to satisfy His own divine wrath as supreme God. Thus, we have done nothing to obtain God's grace or to earn His salvation; all was done by God, who holds all things together and is the essence of everything visible and invisible. For Him, and through Him, everything came into existence.

Church Today: Do not be deceived if you run into a church building that is grand, glorious and filled with hundreds of thousands of people pretending to be true followers of Christ, but the people show no remorse for their actions outside of the church. Do not be shocked by the immorality you may witness in a life that carries a knock off brand of Christ; a name is all that it will be. Do not hold it against Christ if one demonstrates no care in his or her life to be in contact with the rest of the world. Do not be offended if you encounter Christian people with "holier than thou" attitudes because of their own self righteousness.

Such Christians are without Christ, and they will never understand the true meaning of amazing grace. Amazing grace can only be understood accurately when the person is humble enough to acknowledge that we in our best moral and ethical behaviors are like dirty rags before God's holiness.

God's holiness is something that is widely misunderstood, even within the Christian community. Many think that God's holiness is that He is good. The truth is this: while He is good, He is also perfect, not only in the sense that He has no faults, but also because there is no one like Him. He is one of His kind. His love, wisdom, compassion, mercy, justice, passion, even His hate is one of a kind. No man can match His goodness, righteousness and holiness, thus leaving God to be the only one who can be the justification and justifier of our sins before Him.

Job warns us in Job 13:9 "Would it turn out well if He (God) examined you? Could you deceive him as you might deceive a mortal?" (NIV). The point is this, we may fool others, and even ourselves, into believing that we are not wicked like the others, but before God there is no one who is righteous. This is equal to deceiving ourselves and mocking God when we pretend that we are not like others, or worse, when we think we are better than another.

Endnotes

32 Eric Metaxas, Bonhoeffer: Pastor, Martyr, Prophet, Spy, (Thomas Nelson, 2010).

33 Dietrich Bonhoeffer, A Testament to Freedom:The Essential Writings of Dietrich Bonhoeffer, (HarperCollins Publishers, 1990 & 1995).

Chapter 13
The Truth of God and Our Response

It would be very unrealistic if we completely wrote off the evil within us and in this world and told everyone to simply embrace the truth of God and live a life that He desires, and then they might have an abundant life through Christ. We are ancient people with ancient habits, rituals, traditions and ungodly behaviors. The truth is that the evil within us is not going to go away overnight. However, with the appropriate support from others and God's Spirit, it can be managed. The more you are focused on God's truth, the more capable you will be to manage the inner evil, but it will not be obliterated. We must learn to be aware of evil and vigilant for its attempts to betray us, much like we might carefully monitor a chronic infection that can be kept under control if we are careful.[34]

The Truth of Christ: Dietrich Bonhoeffer who lost his life as a result of his participation in an unsuccessful attempt to assassinate Adolph Hitler when he was in his 20s gave a lecture to high school aged crowed, he said:

> One admires Christ according to aesthetic categories as an aesthetic genius, calls him the greatest ethicist; one admires his going to his death as a heroic sacrifice for his ideas. Only one thing one doesn't do: one doesn't take him seriously. That is, one doesn't bring

the center of his or her own life into contact with the claim of Christ to speak the revelation of God and to be that revelation. One maintains a distance between himself or herself and the word of Christ, and allows no serious encounter to take place. I can doubtless live with or without Jesus as a religious genius, as an ethicist, as a gentleman-just as, after all, I can also live without Plato and Kant. ... should, however, there be something in Christ that claims my life entirely with the full seriousness that here God himself speaks and if the word of God once became present only in Christ, then Christ has not only relative but absolute, urgent significance for me. ... Understanding Christ means taking Christ seriously. Understanding this claim means taking seriously his absolute claim on our commitment. And it is now of importance for us to clarify the seriousness of this matter and to extricate Christ from the secularization process in which he has been incorporated since the Enlightenment.[35]

Dietrich Bonhoeffer presents the undeniable truth of Christ with a bold criticism of the unchristian church. He states:

We have articulated a basic criticism of the most grandiose of all human attempts to advance toward the divine-by way of the church. Christianity conceals within itself a germ hostile to the church. It is far too easy for us to base our claims to God on our own Christian religiosity and our church commitment, and in so doing utterly to misunderstand and distort the Christian idea.[36]

You must take baby steps in faith and follow what the Scriptures say. St. Paul writes in Romans 10:9, "If you confess with your mouth that Jesus is Lord and believe in your heart that God raised him from the dead, you will be saved" (ESV). Once you begin your walk with Christ, you will start to understand things that are incomprehensible for you right now. Jesus Christ promised, "But the Helper, the Holy Spirit, whom the Father will send in My name, He will teach you all things, and bring to your remembrance all that I said to you." (John 14:26 NASB). This is when you will be able to "put on the new self, which in the likeness of God has been created in righteousness and holiness of the truth." (Ephesians 4:24 NASB) You will do it not because you have to but because you want to, you will learn to despise the evil ways of your past.

If Not A Church, Then What?: The beauty of the Christian faith lies in the Church that Christ Himself promised in His earthly ministry. He said, "I will build my church; and the gates of hell shall not prevail against it" (Matthew 16:18 NASB). The Church of Jesus Christ is not the building that is made by the human hand, as it is written "The Most High does not dwell in houses made by human hands;" (Acts 7:48 NASB) but in us. Our bodies are the church, St. Paul writes "Do you not know that your body is a temple of the Holy Spirit, who is in you, whom you have received from God? You are not your own" (1 Corinthians 6:9 NASB). The Church is the fellowship of men and women who profess their faith in Jesus Christ. Jesus said, "For where two or three come together in my name, I am there with in the midst of them"(Matthew 18:20 NASB). The Church is also referred to as the body of Christ: "Now you are the body of Christ, and each one of you is a part of it" (I Corinthians 12:27 NIV).

The function of the body of Christ (the Church) is to live not for themselves, but for each other and for Christ. It is the Church that Christ gave His life for and promised to come back, to take her where He has prepared a place for her. Then, there will be no more sorrow, pain nor tears, but joy and everlasting life with an exceptional happiness that is beyond our imagination.

If Not A Religion Then What?: Christ did not come to establish another religion but to provide a way, an escape from the religiosity of man. Religions never accomplished what God wanted from man; God wanted to set man free, but man wanted to engage in practices, traditions, and rituals that made him the prisoner of his own man made faith.

Christ showed the way and paved the path. Christ not only showed the way, but He said "I am the way." He proclaimed the very heart of God, showing by action rather than words that God desires relationships. It is a healthy relationship that involves mutual, unselfish service (as demonstrated by God though Christ on the cross). In a healthy relationship, we change for each other, and in our case it was God who decided in His infinite wisdom to adjust to us. In Christ, He became a limited human being, vulnerable to suffering and death; the Bible says "And being found in appearance as a man, he humbled himself and became obedient to death—even death on a cross!" (Philippians 2:8 NIV).

Bottom line: There is much more that can be said on this topic, but the bottom line is that God, the Creator of this universe, came down from Heaven to Earth, and it is this saving act of God—which is solely due to the work of Jesus Christ on the cross and His resurrection from the dead that brings reconciliation between people and God by making Christ the perfect atonement for our sin.

Invitation

If you believe that Jesus died for a sinner like you and that you need Him in your life, then confess your sins to Him and ask Him to come into your heart and be your Lord and Savior. What do you think? We have all sinned and deserve God's judgment. God our Father sent His only Son to satisfy His judgment for those who believe in Him. Jesus, the Creator and eternal Son of God who lived a sinless life, loves us so much that He died for our sins, taking the punishment that we deserve, was buried, and rose from the dead, according to the Bible. If you truly believe and trust this in your heart, receiving Jesus alone as your Savior declaring, "Jesus is Lord," then you will be saved from judgment, and you will spend eternity with God in heaven.

Endnotes

34 Gordon MacDonald, Rebuilding Your Broken World (Nashvill: Thomas Nelson Publishers,2003), 84.

35 Dietrich Bonhoeffer, Barcelona Lectures, December 11, 1928.

36 Clifford J. Green and Michael DeJonge, Th Bonhoeffer Reader (Minneapolis: Fortress Press, 2013), 68.

Part Four
Jesus the Nazarene

Chapter 14
Jesus Among Other Men?

We live in a time where an immense amount of information is available at the touch of a button. The Internet has brought the whole world together to share ideas, philosophies, and religious beliefs. In our global village, one thing that has constantly been questioned and brought under scrutiny is the Christian claim that "Jesus is the only way." The Western society once embraced Christianity exclusively is not only moving away from Christianity but also experimenting with all kinds of ideas and religions. Much of that can be credited to the advancement of our society of the Internet. The challenge again comes from the proponents of relativism. The question asked is very simple: "If you make one religion superior over the others will it not cause war in the name of religion?"

History: Recent history has witnessed massacres in the name of religion; however, history has also witnessed charity, piety, compassion, and care by religious people. Faith-based non-profit organizations have made a huge difference in the lives of millions. War or massacres in the name of religion can not rightfully be associated with Christianity, surely not with the teachings of Christ. We can call Jesus the "founder" of Christianity, in the sense that the religious movement began with Him and is associated with Him. Neither Jesus nor other leaders of Christianity ever encouraged believers to take over other lands or pillage others in the name of Christ. Contrary to exuding hate, violence, and superiority over others, Jesus preached humility, mercy, love, compassion, care, and forgiveness in words and actions.

While He was beaten and dragged to the cross unjustly, Jesus said, "Father, forgive them that they do not know what they are doing" (Luke 23:34 NIV). That the "last will be first, and the first will be last" (Matthew 20:16 NIV) is a teaching that clearly changed the focus of humanity from a search for power in this world a search for power in the next world; and "Anyone who has two shirts should share with the one who has none, and anyone who has food should do the same" (Luke 3:11 NIV) became the foundation for sharing and caring for others, regardless of their gender, race, ethnicity or religious practice. Jesus's teachings make him the first humanitarian and philanthropist who warned his disciples that "those of you who do not give up everything you have cannot be my disciples" (Luke 14:33 NTL). Love of material possession leads to uncontrollable desires for power, which then leads to war and bloodshed.

Jesus's teachings were not anything but love. He taught and demanded from his followers nothing but the highest standards for ethics, purity, and, above all, how to treat others. He set the foundation for perfect peace that will be attained eventually in the unfolding of God's eternal plan for us. Jesus said,

> *Do not judge, or you too will be judged. For in the same way you judge others, you will be judged, and with the measure you use, it will be measured to you. Why do you look at the speck of sawdust in your brother's eye and pay no attention to the plank in your own eye? How can you say to your brother, 'Let me take the speck out of your eye,' when all the time there is a plank in your own eye? You hypocrite, first take the plank out of your own eye, and then you will see*

*clearly to remove the speck from your brother's eye.
(Matthew 7:1-5 NIV).*

He also said, "You have heard that it was said, 'YOU SHALL
LOVE YOUR NEIGHBOR and hate your enemy.' But I say to
you, love your enemies and pray for those who persecute you,"
(Matthew 5:43-44 NASB).

Before Christianity, the Romans were happy with their gods.
They were happy to swap each other's gods on a daily basis. A
problem arose when Christians started claiming that Jesus is the
only way. Logically, what Christians were saying was that there is
no other valid god and no other religion but Christ. Today, Christianity is confronted with neo-liberals in the church of Christ,
When you ask them what they think about the idea that "Jesus
is the only way," they answer that they cannot judge others. It is
understandable that a Christian should not judge others by what
they believe or practice, but that is certainly not an excuse to
water down the exclusiveness of Christ or to deny it all together.
Right at that moment, they have denied Christ and Christianity in
order to receive the approval of others. Historically, true Christians have always laid down their lives for the uncompromising
truth of the Gospel, that Jesus is the only way. Christ said, "But
whosoever shall deny me before men, him will I also deny before
my father which is in heaven" (Matthew 10:33 KJV).

Rational: Rationally speaking, what is true is true. No matter
how you dissect the truth, it will always reveal truth. Regardless
of how much a person lies in their own life, no one likes to be
lied to. Truth is inevitably demanded more than it is actually
practiced. The truth may have only one right answer and many
wrong answers. 2+2=4 and can never be 5, 9, 36 or any other
number. Thus, truth is narrow and hard to accept at its face value
because what is not true will have many paths leading to it, but

only one path will lead to the truth. In other words, for every right answer, there are many wrong answers. Therefore, people would generally rather pick and choose the pseudo-truth to meet their desired outcomes.

One of the reasons why people generally do not want to hear Christian claims about Christ's exclusiveness is because they think that Christians have made up the story of Christ's death and resurrection. If someone does not believe in His death and resurrection, he or she would not come to the truth that is the basis of Christianity. A reasonable question would be "How would one really know that the claims that Christianity makes are true, since other religions make the exact same claims?" Lee Strobel, a former investigation journalist at the Chicago tribune and author of the *New York Times* Best-Selling Book, *The Case for Christ*, provides a number of compelling evidences as a part of his journey from a skeptic to a sincere seeker to a bold witness of Jesus Christ. His conclusion about the story of Jesus as it is mentioned in the four Gospels is nothing more than a simple truth that is testable and verifiable. He gives five 'E's that I intend to expand upon in the next chapter. Lee and I would both say that the Execution of Jesus Christ, the Empty Tomb of Jesus Christ, the Eye Witness of Jesus Christ, Early Records about Jesus Christ, and the Emergence of the Christian Church are more than enough evidence to prove the truth of Jesus's story and the superiority of Christianity over all other religions. A skeptic mind will demand more than just a few simple fables that are being told and retold, generation after generation; what can really convince one's mind and heart is entirely up to that person. People were skeptics when it was first told that the earth is not flat and that it revolves around the sun. Regardless of the overwhelming evidence for this scientific fact, for a long time people did not accept the truth, and even today there are parts of the world where people refute this truth.

Chapter 15
The Evidence that Makes Jesus the Only Way

One thing that I have learned from traveling, observing, writing and speaking to people throughout the world over the past two decades is that people are diverse even within a country and society. Their diversity can be observed in many ways-socially, economically, racially, ethnically, culturally, religiously, and intellectually, for example. Thus, no matter what we say, we are different from each other. This difference is good, but it can be bad when we fail to acknowledge it. The fact that our diversity can influence our thought processes cannot be regarded as a matter of indifference when we are investigating among truth-like answers.

In the case of Jesus Christ, His exclusiveness may be considered hurtful to many who seek access to God's kingdom (a glorious place that we all desire in the afterlife, where we would be happy and live in peace for eternity) through different paths, such as moral goodness, yoga, dedication to different religious rituals and teachings, or living a selfless life while not following any organized religion. It makes perfect sense if we take an unbiased look at the following evidences, setting aside our intellectual, and religious barriers that can taint the purity of the truth.

Evidence #1—Execution: There are a number of widely circulated theories about Christ's execution that differ from the popular story (Christ died by crucifixion and was buried under the supervision and security of Roman guards). The only way to reasonably evaluate the truth is to look at the facts: 1) The Roman guards testified that Christ had died; 2) The Jewish religious leaders who demanded Jesus's execution through crucifixion would have certainly made sure that He was dead before letting Him be buried; 3) The people, including Joseph of Arimathea was a member of the Sanhedrin helped in the burial of Jesus Christ; finally, 4) if Christ had not been executed, dead, and buried, then there never would have been any mention of an empty tomb.

Evidence #2—Empty Tomb: Today, 2,000 years after the event, the empty tomb does not mean much, but, at the time, it stood as a strong witness that Christ had indeed risen. His disciples led with that argument, stating that they have the tombs of Abraham, David, and others with their bodies still in them, but Jesus's tomb was empty. The crucifixion and resurrection of Jesus Christ was not an unknown event in first century Israel. The news was so big that, if it would have happened during the twenty first century, it would have made front page news.

There are two major theories that are presented by the unbelievers:

1. Someone must have stolen Jesus's body.

2. The women and disciples went to the wrong tomb.

There is a problem with both theories.

The Problem with Theory No. 1: It assumes that disciples were some sort of warriors who overcame the Roman guards of the tomb (who were known as the best soldiers at that time) and stole the body. Neither the Romans nor the Jews would have stolen the body because they had no motive to do so. The problem is Jesus's disciples were not only not warriors, but they abandoned their leaders and hid.

The Problem with Theory No. 2: It assumes that the women who found the tomb empty were mistaken and did not go to the right tomb in the first place. These were the women who had watched Jesus being laid away; they were heartbroken and wanted to be there at the tomb, but they were told to come back after the Sabbath. They not only knew the location of the tomb, but they were discussing a practical issue way to enter the tomb. It is written that they said amongst themselves, "Who will roll away the stone from the door of the tomb for us?" This question shows that they were not expecting to find an empty tomb; thus, there was no desire to produce a story of the resurrected Christ as a result of a wishful thinking. Note that the stone was not rolled away to let Jesus out. According to John 20:19, Jesus, in His resurrected body, could pass through material barriers; thus, the only reason why the stone was rolled away was so that others could see in and be persuaded that Jesus Christ had indeed risen from the dead. It was meant to be evidence for all generations.

Moreover, if either theory had been true, then the Jews or Romans would have produced the body and closed the case for good. The early morning of the first Easter Sunday proves both of these theories wrong, and as yet another attempt to suppress the truth. Also, if Jesus's body had been stolen, His burial cloths would not have been left neatly folded inside, which further proves that His rising was not merely the act of grave robbers.

Evidence #3—Eye Witness: Jesus appeared to over 500 different people post-resurrection. Many myths mention "someone" who heard or who saw Jesus, and so the myths began. But the recorded resurrection accounts names specific people—Mary, Peter, Paul, and others who encountered Christ personally. The first eyewitnesses were women, which is very significant considering the history and authenticity of Jesus's story. No ancient author would have used women as the prime witnesses to Christ's resurrection to fabricate facts, especially considering the controversy and religious significance of the event. This further proves the accuracy of eye witnesses accounts, regardless of the insignificance of women as witnesses in Biblical times. This prevents male Gospel writers from hiding the fact that the first witnesses to the resurrection were women, and it also shows how God in Christ validated the equality of women and man by honoring the former with this important role.

Paul's testimony in 1 Corinthians 15:6 is another place of incredible evidence. Paul wrote the letter around 55 AD and quotes many of the 500 men and women who saw the risen Jesus Christ. Today, there is a theory that all of the witnesses were victims of hallucination, and this theory has been medically disproven. Psychologists say that it is impossible for such a large crowd of people to hallucinate at once, and, besides, no one claimed that they saw Jesus physically in his resurrected body after ascending into Heaven, which likely would have happened if these witnesses had been merely hallucinating.

Evidence #4—Early Records (the church creed): Myths take time to develop, many years or even decades. But the news of Christ's resurrection spread within months. The Church creed, as soon as the Church was founded declared the exclusiveness of Jesus Christ as the only way, who came, died, and rose again and will one day come to judge the entire world. Early records about Jesus's story include not only the four Gospels, but also the works of many historians, Josephus, Tacitus, Pliny the Younger, to name a few.

Evidence #5—Emergence: An undeniable truth about the story of Jesus Christ mentioned in the four Gospels is the emergence of the Church. After the arrest and crucifixion of Jesus

Christ, His disciples hid themselves behind locked doors. They were terrified that they might meet the same fate as Jesus. However, no one can object that something drastic happened that soon changed them all from cowards to bold preachers of Jesus's Gospel. What else could account for the rapid growth of the church at that time? Some say the disciples duped the people, but those same disciples died defending the very truth that they preached-that Jesus Christ was alive. Only a few weeks after the resurrection of Christ, Peter spoke to 3,000 people, presenting his argument, " Fellow Israelites, listen to this: Jesus of Nazareth was a man accredited by God to you by miracles, wonders and signs, which God did among you through him, as you yourselves know. This man was handed over to you by God's deliberate plan and foreknowledge; and you, with the help of wicked men, put him to death by nailing him to the cross. But God raised him from the dead, freeing him from the agony of death, because it was impossible for death to keep its hold on him... Therefore let all Israel be assured of this: God has made this Jesus, whom you crucified, both Lord and Messiah" (Acts 2:29-34, 36 NIV) If it had been false, they would have told him so to his face. However, it says "Those who accepted his message were baptized, and about three thousand were added to their number that day" (Acts 2:41 NIV). It is true that countless people have died for Jesus, and that the resurrection of Jesus Christ is a widely accepted historical fact. No one died in a fight to conquer the world for Jesus; They died believing that the risen Christ was their strength and hope.

Chapter 16
The Origin of Christ's Exclusiveness

The exclusivity of Jesus Christ in the Christian faith has consistently been an issue throughout modern history. Since the dawn of Christianity, it has been considered a scandal. As a matter of fact, the Christian faith has always been a scandal. One can trace the roots of opposition from the day when Christ started preaching His message; it was the cause of His crucifixion and the cause of death for millions after Him who believed in His message. There are a few simple answers to the question, "What makes Jesus the only way?" because the exclusivity of Christ is not based on personal beliefs but on various authentic claims about Him.

Claim # 1—Jesus's claim about Himself: Jesus's claim about His exclusiveness can be read in John 14:6: "I am the way and the truth and the life. No one comes to the Father except through me" (NIV). Jesus was considered a Jewish teacher, even by His own enemies. Masses of people were amazed by His teachings. From day one, His bold, clear, yet simple teachings held the attention of the masses. What brought division among the people was His outrageous claims about Himself. In the Gospel of Luke 4:16-29, we see Jesus's first claim about Himself as the Messiah, the divine one that the Jewish people were waiting for. In a synagogue, He was given the scroll of the prophet Isaiah, and He read the prophecy about the Messiah. In verse 21 we find He claims, "Today this Scripture has been fulfilled in your hearing." The response He received was not surprising; Verses 28-29 read, "All the people in the synagogue were furious when they heard this. They got up, drove him out of the town, and took him to the brow of the hill on which the town was built, in order to throw him off the cliff" (NIV). It was in the beginning of Jesus's earthly ministry; He would make many similar claims throughout the three and a half years of His ministry on earth. Jesus made one of His last claims at the Festival of Dedication in Jerusalem. It was winter, and Jesus was in the temple courts, walking in Solomon's Colonnade.

The Jews there gathered around Him, saying,

"How long will you keep us in suspense? If you are the Messiah, tell us plainly," Jesus answered, "I did tell you, but you do not believe. The works I do in my Father's name testify about me, but you do not believe because you are not my sheep. My sheep listen to my voice; I know them, and they follow me. I give them eternal life, and they shall never perish; no one will snatch them out of my hand. My Father, who has given them to me, is greater than all; no one can snatch them out of my Father's hand. I and the Father are one" (John 10:15-30 NIV).

Again his Jewish opponents picked up stones to stone him, but Jesus said to them, "I have shown you many good works from the Father. For which of these do you stone me?" "We are not stoning you for any good work," they replied, "but for blasphemy, because you, a mere man, claim to be God" (John 10:22-33 NIV). He knew His claim would upset the religious leadership of His time; He also knew that people would not understand His claims. This is precisely why He never used such blunt language as, "I am the son of God." He gave ample evidence that He was and is the son of God. Note that, Jewish religious leaders knew and understood exactly who Jesus was claiming to be, and this is precisely what we see in John 10:33, "We are not stoning you for any good work," they replied, "but for blasphemy, because you, a mere man, claim to be God" (NLT).

Claim #2—The disciples' claim about Jesus: If followers truly believe their leader, they must proclaim what they have witnessed so that others might know the truth about them. However, when it comes to Jesus's disciples, we see a unique situation arise. The disciples were not sure what to believe when Jesus was crucified. Although Jesus taught them in secret who He was before going to the cross, His disciples' faith was still not strong enough to understand the suffering of their Messiah. Their dreams were shattered when, rather than over throwing the Roman government and bringing about a full reign of God, Jesus was arrested like a criminal and hung on the cross. The mental and emotional trauma that they went through must have been very difficult one. It was the resurrection of Jesus Christ that revitalized their understanding of His teachings and claims. It was then that the convincing evidence of the resurrection made them into a group of people who proclaimed fearlessly, boldly and uncompromisingly that Jesus is the only way. If they had not used the definite article "the" then they would have saved their lives and the lives of their loved ones. They died for what they believed in-the life, death and resurrection of Jesus Christ. It was not blind obedience or simply the following of a leader that made the disciples willfully give their lives; it was the convincing evidence of Jesus's resurrection that radicalized their whole being, convincing them that it was useless and utterly meaningless to live a life hiding the truth of Jesus Christ.

Claim #3—The Scriptural claims about Jesus: There are many examples throughout history of people making false claims about their identities, over a period of time, their reality is exposed, and they fail to leave a mark on this world. There have also been cases throughout history where men claim to be God, yet their lack of control over death has proved them to be liars every time. Within the Jewish Scriptures, one can find hundreds of prophecies about the Messiah. There was always confusion among Jewish scholars about many of these prophecies because these prophecies reflected two Messiahs. Therefore, some thought it might be two different people; however, after the resurrection of Jesus Christ, it became very clear that all of the prophecies were talking about the same Messiah who will appear at two different times. The first is the suffering Messiah, referring to the first coming of Jesus Christ, and the second is the warrior and judge Messiah, as is promised in the New Testament.

According to a scholarly estimate, Jesus Christ fulfilled 351 prophecies, and other sources claimed that Jesus fulfilled as many as 700 plus prophecies.[37] Most of these prophecies were fulfilled at Jesus' birth, during His ministry on earth, at His death on the Cross, and His resurrection. Now skeptics believe that some of these instances occurred merely by chance, and others were caused by intentional efforts. However, Dr. Peter Stoner[38] conducted a mathematical study to see what are the odds were of Jesus fulfilling all of these prophecies. He estimated that one person could reasonably accomplish just 48 of the 300 or so Old Testament prophecies. He calculated the odds at 1 in 10 to the 157th power. That is one in 10,000,000,000,000,000,000,000,000,000,000,000,000,000,000,000,000,0 00. According to Emile Borel, a leading authority on the probability theory, once we go past 10 to the 50th power, the probabilities are so small that it is almost impossible to think that they will occur.[39] The chances that one person can fulfill all of those prophecies are mathematically impossible to think of, but Jesus Christ fulfilled them all.

Claim #4—The miracles and deeds He performed: Miracles are supernatural phenomena. In modern Western culture, miracles are ridiculed and the argument of miracles as the evidence of Jesus's holiness is publicly mocked. However, in ancient times, miracles were not only common but they were highly respected, just as they are today in the Eastern world. Many religious figures performed miracles. In the story of Moses and the Pharaoh, Moses performed miracles alongside the Pharaoh's servants. However, in Jesus's case, the miracles He performed were not only different, but they were also performed in a noticeably unique way. He performed these miracles with power and authority, as if they were His own and not borrowed from someone else. This is why His opponents never objected to the power of His miracles, just challenged the demonstration of them. They said, "We are not stoning you for any good work," they replied, "but for blasphemy, because you, a mere man, claim to be God" (John 10:22-33 NIV).

Endnotes

37 Jack Wellman, "What are the Odds of Jesus' 700 Plus Prophecies Fulfillment?" Yahoo Voice, December 12, 2009 http://voices.yahoo.com/what-odds-jesus-700-plus-prophecies-fulfillment-5064980.html?cat=6 (accessed June 27, 2014).

38 Peter W. Stoner, Science Speaks (Chicago: Moody Bible Institute, 1968), 333.

39 Emile Borel, Probability and Life, Dover Publications, translated from the original, Les Probabilite et la Vie (New York:Dover Publications, 1962).

Chapter 17
Historicity of Jesus

One of the easiest ways to attempt to discredit the word or evidence of a witness is by simply denying the existence of the topic at hand. No matter how many witnesses are presented, and no matter what evidence they provide, it is all for nothing if someone is bound and determined to prove that the story as told never took place.

One of the most commonly used tactics to deny the overwhelming proof regarding Jesus's claim that He is to be the only way is a diversionary tactic, claiming that Jesus never existed. What if He never lived? The idea is to avoid dealing with the proof of Jesus's exclusivity and to get rid of Him all together. C. S. Lewis' presents an idea in his book, *Mere Christianity*, either Jesus was who He said He was, which means that Jesus was telling the truth (and therefore is the only way), or He thought that He was the Messiah and told people, but he was wrong (and, therefore a lunatic), or He knew He was not what He told people He was, but he said it anyway (and, therefore, is a liar). This theory provides grounds to discuss Jesus as a divine being on the basis of His existence, contrary to the belief of many non Christians that He lived in the first century and was just a good, human teacher and nothing more. Attempts to prove or disprove the existence of Jesus Christ has ignited whole new debate that is pushing back the progress Christian scholars have made in the last 2,000 years to present the case of Jesus's exclusiveness. It is as if a case almost came to its conclusion, and, right before the verdict, a trick was played, and the clock was rolled back 2,000 years.

The question of Jesus's existence is neither morally right nor intellectually respectful, yet the question is valid regardless of the intentions of the skeptics and critics of Christianity. How do we know that Jesus of Nazareth really existed as it is believed and professed by billions of Christians and non-Christians?

One of the best places to start is the Gospel accounts, and although one might raise allegations as to the authenticity of the writers, the truth is that from the beginning of the Church, Christians were targeted for what they believed and claimed they witnessed. The gospel of Luke might be an excellent place to start because he starts his account with these words:

> *"Many have undertaken to draw up an account of the things that have been fulfilled among us, just as they were handed down to us by those who from the first were eyewitnesses and servants of the word. With this in mind, since I myself have carefully investigated everything from the beginning, I too decided to write an orderly account for you, most excellent Theophilus, so that you may know the certainty of the things you have been taught." (Luke 1:1-4 NIV)*

As a credible historian and well educated man, Luke not only penned the Gospel of Luke as an orderly account, but he also recorded much of the history of Paul's missionary work and of the ministries of the first church in the first century. His gospel is based on interviews with eyewitnesses and the servants of the Word.

In Acts 3, Peter, one of the apostles who denied having any association with Christ the night Jesus was arrested, hid himself with other disciples after the arrest and death of Jesus, and went back to work after Christ's death. Upon witnessing the risen Christ, Peter spoke boldly before thousands of People in Jerusalem. He was plain and direct:

> *Fellow Israelites, listen to this: Jesus of Nazareth was a man accredited by God to you by miracles, wonders and signs, which God did among you through him, as you yourselves know. This man was handed over to you by God's deliberate plan and foreknowledge; and you, with the help of wicked men, put him to death by nailing him to the cross. But God raised him from the dead, freeing him from the agony of death, because it was impossible for death to keep its hold on him (Acts 3:22-24 NIV).*

The audience included Jews and Gentiles, but none of them said Peter was wrong, or that Jesus never existed. Chapter 7 says, "Therefore let all Israel be assured of this: God has made this Jesus, whom you crucified, both Lord and Messiah," and the result was amazing, "about three thousand were added to their number that day." These converts were the same people who were accusing him and the rest of the apostles of being drunk, but upon hearing the truth and realizing what they did to Jesus, they repented and accepted Christ.

Jesus was well known for His miraculous healing His powerful and authoritative teaching, for standing up to the religious hypocrisy of Israel, and as a rebel who made people act in a way that was not approved or appreciated by the religious leaders. In a story about two men traveling home, Luke writes, "And behold, two of them were going that very day to a village named Emmaus, which was about seven miles from Jerusalem. And they were talking with each other about all these things that had taken place. While they were talking and discussing, Jesus

Himself approached and began traveling with them" (Luke 23:13-15 NASB). Luke must have interviewed them to record their exact account, and the geographical information provides extra authenticity as corroborating evidence. It has been archeologically proven that such a place existed in the first century.

Luke would have taken all of the necessary measures that a good historian or researcher would have taken in order to publish authentic work, especially work connected to a well-known public figure like Jesus. It would be exactly as if I were to write something about our current President of the United States. Do you not think that people who read my work would immediately critique any discrepancies that they may find? However, in this case, not only the Gospel of Luke and Acts, but all four of the Gospels and the Epistles were widely accepted as legitimate accounts of Jesus Christ. Out of thousands of accounts written in the first three centuries, only these four Gospels- Matthew, Mark, Luke and John were considered to be authentic, as early Christians felt that these four books alone contained the most vital factual information. No other books survived, simply because they were either insignificant or could not stand up to the true story of Jesus Christ in any way. What was true and what was believed to be true survived, and the rest perished.

Chapter 18
What if Jesus was a Myth?

Greek mythology is intriguing, but it is not necessarily truthful. Nevertheless today, people are neither expected to believe in Greek myths, nor are they necessarily mocked if they choose to believe in them wholeheartedly. When we read about mythological characters and their stories, no matter how impressed we are with the creativity of the writing, we know that it cannot be true. However, if our intentions are to investigate the truth, then we must follow simple guidelines.

In the question of Jesus Christ as a mythical being, we must follow simple guidelines:

1. Are there exaggerations in ancient tales of Jesus's teachings and actions, including some that are unseen or unheard of?

2. Was any part of the story fabricated to imitate the first century Jewish community, in the Roman province of Palestine?

3. In answer to number two, the places mentioned in the accounts of Jesus are real places that were indeed part of the Roman province of Palestine in the first century.

4. Do historical documents talk about the places and events that are mentioned in the Gospels account of Jesus Christ?

5. Does archeological evidence prove the existences of places, people groups, and events in the four Gospels?

6. Are there accounts by the Roman government, Jewish scholars, or from sources other than the Gospels?

There an answer for each and every one the points above. To start, even the Gospels not recognized by the early church, (such as the Gospel of Thomas, The Gospel of Judas, or the Gospel of Phillip) do not refute the existence of Christ. They base their story on the person of Jesus, but still they are not authentic Gospels. The Jewish historian Josephus, who wrote a comprehensive history of the Jewish people near the end of the first century, records the martyrdom of James, calling him "the brother of Jesus who was called Christ." Again, this authenticates the belief that Christians still practice today. This passage is considered by most historians and scholars to genuine and true. This is an important piece of proof that someone named Jesus actually lived in the first century and that some considered Him to be the Messiah.

Josephus wrote another, more controversial passage:

About this time came Jesus, a wise man, if indeed it is appropriate to call him a man. For he was a performer of paradoxical feats, a teacher of people who accept the unusual with pleasure, and he won over many of the Jews and also many Greeks. He was the Christ. When Pilate, upon the accusation of the first men amongst us, condemned him to be crucified, those who had formerly loved him did not cease to follow him, for he appeared to them on the third day, living again, as the divine prophets foretold, along with a myriad of other marvelous things concerning him. And the tribe of the Christians, so named after him, has not disappeared to this day.[40]

In the Annals of Tacitus, Tacitus reveals how Nero, in an effort to hide his crime in which he planned a fire that destroyed most of Rome, used Christians as a scapegoat. He writes:

> *Consequently, to get rid of the report, Nero fastened the guilt and inflicted the most exquisite tortures on a class hated for their abominations, called Christians by the populace. Christus, from whom the name had its origin, suffered the extreme penalty during the reign of Tiberius at the hands of one of our procurators, Pontius Pilatus, and a most mischievous superstition, thus checked for the moment, again broke out not only in Judaea, the first source of the evil, but even in Rome, where all things hideous and shameful from every part of the world find their centre and become popular.*[41]

There are many other direct and indirect references to Jesus Christ and to the people who worshipped Christ rather than the Emperor. Not only are the events, people groups, and places mentioned in the Gospels real and attested by other literature outside Christian books, but modern day archeological evidence has now made them unquestionable.

It is interesting and plausible that, among all religions and faiths, Christianity is the only faith that invites people to go and test everything about Jesus for themselves. Scientists are welcome to measure the depth and length of the accounts of the four Gospels that present the true story of Jesus, skeptics are welcome to investigate on their own about the historical Jesus, and religious people are welcome to analyze Jesus's teachings.

To read more about the historical evidence of the person of Jesus, please see chapter 29-30 on the persecution of early

Christians due to their faith in the person of Christ. Their persecution was recorded by the persecutors.

Endnotes

40 There is still much debate over the authenticity of this passage. The current consensus is that Josephus did write something about Jesus here, but that later edits were made by a follower of Christ. The parts in bold italics are those parts which are commonly believed to be later edits, for there is evidence that Josephus was not a follower of Christ and would not have characterized Him in this way. The description of Jesus as a "wise man" and "teacher" are more consistent with Josephus' style and vocabulary found elsewhere in his work, and are probably the actual descriptions he used. (Evidence for Jesus Outside the Bible by Michael Lane)

41 Tacitus, "The Annals of Tacitus" Early Christian Writings, http://www.early-christianwritings.com/text/annals.html (accessed June 25, 2014).

Chapter 19
Death of Jesus the Nazarene

Many people try to disprove the death of Jesus Christ in order to disprove the resurrection story. The Christian faith is based on a few simple doctrines:

- Man is saved by grace alone.
- Atonement: Jesus paid the price for our sins in full. He purchased us by giving Himself up to be crucified.
- We are all sinners and the wages of sin is death, consequently, all of us are destined to die—an eternal death.
- The death of Jesus Christ on the cross provided redemption thus, the cross became the pivotal point in the post-Christ crucifixion.

Many theories have been raised to discredit the biblical account of Jesus' death. In modern times, the theories take an apologetic approach to raise doubts. The following are a couple of examples.

The first theory to discredit the biblical account of Jesus's death: There is considerable controversy about how intertwined the four Gospels are. In particular, some of the stories are word for word. Rather than being four independent accounts, they may just be a mishmash of perspectives from different writers. There are very few passages in Mark that are not found in a either Matthew or Luke.

The aim of this argument is to raise doubts over whether the four Gospels were in fact a copy of the same account. Although it is almost universally thought that Matthew and Luke had access to the Gospel of Mark, there is clear evidence from the accounts of all four Gospels that each perspective was different from the others. There are some significant portions of both Matthew and Luke that are not related in any way to Mark's account. The four Gospels give an extensive, independent look into the life of Jesus, His teachings, and His death. So, while in their individual materials they do not provide the full picture, in collaboration they do. The Gospel of John is so unlike the accounts from Matthew, Mark, and Luke that virtually every scholar believes it to be independent from them. So within the first century, we have four independent accounts of Jesus's life and death.

In the end, these allegations only serve to strengthen the Christian claim of the unity of the accounts. However, it needs to be said that each writer had very distinctive theological angles that they wanted to highlight. Matthew's focus was to provide a theological understanding of the relationship of Christianity and Judaism as clear as he could; Mark's angle was that of the suffering servant, the Messiah; Luke's focus was to provide a theological understanding of what Jesus, His ministry, His death and His resurrection meant for the poor and socially concerned; John presents Jesus as the divine man and Son of God.

The second theory to discredit the biblical account of Jesus' death: The disciples' conviction that they had seen the risen Christ is notable. Under circumstances of great conviction and belief, there is a natural tendency of people to distort reality and convince themselves and others of events that may not be true. The point would be much more convincing if there were an account of a non-disciple or non-believer who had also witnessed the empty tomb and resurrection.

Let me start by answering this allegation from bottom to top: Would you take the word of an eye witness who did not meet or see Jesus, but had simply heard about Him from a secondary source? Besides, we do have a number of accounts where the authors were not disciples. It is also important to note that the Gospel of Luke was written by Luke who a historian who wrote based on facts and stories he collected right after the resurrection of Jesus Christ. He was not a direct disciple of Jesus Christ.

It is quite possible that our conviction and loyalty to someone makes us distort the truth and provides a somewhat more predictable story. However, in the case of Jesus Christ, there are many reasons why the disciples would not have committed such an ungodly act, here are a few:

Reason No. 1: What would they have gained by doing so? Only rejection, persecution and death. This is precisely what happened to all but one disciple, although he was persecuted too. It makes sense for someone to willfully present a false or a compromised story if he will be benefited, but it really does not make sense to distort the story of Jesus, doing so would likely lead to their death or the death of their loved ones.

Reason No. 2: Someone who is campaigning for a political office and asks his followers to make him look good, is often distorting the facts. However, neither Jesus nor His followers were trying to gain political power; especially in Jesus's case, his followers presented a very controversial story that certainly had the potential to make Jesus less popular among the religious and political community.

We also must remember that they honored and respected Jesus so much that it prompted them to record His life with great integrity. That was the only way that they would have showed their love for Him. Another scholar, Blomberg put this way, "Besides, these disciples had nothing to gain except criticism, ostracism, and martyrdom. They certainly had nothing to win financially. If anything, this would have provided pressure to keep quiet, to deny Jesus, to downplay him, even to forget they never met him yet because of their integrity, they proclaimed what they saw, even when it meant suffering and death."[42]

Reason No. 3: The point that women could not serve as legal witnesses due to their inferior legal and social status is incorrect. Women could indeed be legal witnesses as long as there was no male present at the time (so at least we know they had a good legal system. Since there were no men present at the supposed discovery of the empty tomb, there is nothing significant about the women in the story.

This allegation is counterproductive. The presence of women was not merely to prove the empty tomb, the empty tomb stood for itself as evidence. The Gospel writers, however, did not fail to acknowledge that it was women who witnessed the empty tomb first; because women, as second-class citizens, were more bold than the male disciples to go and visit the tomb on the Easter Sunday morning. Besides, no one has any doubt that, in societies where women do not have an equal voice to men, it is not a good idea to place a woman as the prime witness.

Reason No. 4: The flourishing of Jesus's story (and the need to prove it) in a Jewish controlled city suggests that there was significant hostility towards Christians from the Jews. In fact, at the time, Christianity was considered a strange, and unimportant cult that obtained its followers from the lower rung of society and, thus, did not merit all that much consideration. The lack of suppression and the attempts to disprove the resurrection story could well have been due to simple indifference (after the supposed death of Jesus, the Jewish authorities probably thought they had won, and Christianity would fizzle out before long). It would be almost 100 years before Christianity would be taken seriously.

This allegation simply proves the point that Christians were first considered a Jewish sect and a cult and that Jewish authorities took all necessary measures to crush Christianity. Nevertheless, despite the horrendous actions against those who decided to follow Jesus and believe in His resurrection, Christianity survived, prospered, and spread all over the world.

Endnotes

42 Blomber, Craig. "The Historical Reliability of the New Testament." In Reasonable Faith, by William Lane Criag, 193-231. Westchester, Ill.: Crossway, 1994.

Chapter 20
The Resurrection of Jesus Christ

Before we discuss the proof of Jesus's resurrection, we need to understand the skeptics' questions regarding Jesus's death. Based on two of the verses from the Gospel of Mark 15:36, and 44 it is believed by conspiracy theorists that Jesus must not have died at all because Pilate seemed surprised at his quick death. However, they fail to examine the condition of Jesus's body. The torture He received before going to the cross must have ushered Him into a quick death. The same argument has taken many shapes over the last hundreds of years; it is basically believed by these theorists that, when He was taken down from the cross, He must have been resuscitated, and, thus, a resurrection never took place.

Stress and Anxiety: One can imagine the pain he or she to go through right before being executed. The stress and anxiety would increase as the hour drew nearer would come from and shame and humiliation the very people for whom you were giving your life. As a human being, Jesus was such a man. He one day publicly asked if there was anyone who could provide an account of any sin in His life. Not one could raise an allegation. He also asked His opponents why they persecuted Him, and the answer was simply that He, a mere man, claimed to be God. He never refuted or rejected such a notion, and He never refused His position on His divine origin.

The Garden of Gethsemane became the battleground of His flesh (fully man) and His sprit (fully God). He prayed before His father, and the Gospel accounts tell that Jesus began to sweat blood. Medical doctors verify that intense stress and severe anxiety can cause the release of chemicals that break down the capillaries in the sweat glands. As a result, a small amount of blood creeps into these glands, and the sweat comes out tinged with blood.

Tortures Night and Day: According to medical experts, such a medical condition should have a severe impact on the rest of the body. Primarily, the skin will become extremely fragile. This is why, after the long night of torture and no sleep, His body was not in shape to take a beating the next morning. However, as history tells us, the Roman soldiers were not sympathetic to criminals nor to those that they perceived to be criminals. The next day, when Jesus was flogged by them, His skin would not have had the strength to endure such pain. Now remember the flogging was done in an effort to please the Jewish leadership, in hopes of torturing Jesus but still keeping him alive. The extreme suffering carried out by a terribly brutal whip and the will of a solider delivering 39 lashes would have left no energy in Jesus's body, and His body must have been dragged by the soldiers from one court room to another.

Flogging Device and Scourging Practices: The Roman flogging device was a short whip called a flagrum, with lead balls and sheep bones tied into leather thongs. When a naked victim was tied to a flogging post and was hit with the device, it left a deep stripe-like laceration that caused massive bleeding and was usually associated with considerable blood loss. Now, combine the effect of the Roman flogging with the previous night, when the anxiety and stress had made Jesus's body so sensitive that blood was creeping into the sweat glands. Christ also endured scourging, which was when a man was stripped of his clothing, and his hands were tied to an upright post. The back, buttocks, and legs were flogged either by two soldiers (lictors) or by one who alternated positions. The severity of the scourging depended on the disposition of the lictors and was intended to weaken the victim to a state just short of collapse or death. After the scourging, the soldiers often taunted their victim.[43]

Medical Aspects of Scourging: As the Roman soldiers repeatedly struck the victim's back with full force, the iron balls would cause deep contusions, and the leather thongs and sheep bones would cut into the skin and subcutaneous tissues. Then, as the flogging continued, the lacerations would tear into the underlying skeletal muscles and produce quivering ribbons of bleeding flesh. Pain and blood loss generally set the stage for circulatory shock. The extent of blood loss may well have determined how long the victim would survive on the cross.

Scourging of Jesus: At the Praetorium, Jesus was severely whipped. (Although the severity of the scourging is not discussed in the four Gospel accounts, it is implied in one of the epistles (1Peter 2:24). A detailed word study of the ancient Greek text for this verse indicates that the scourging of Jesus was particularly harsh.) It is not known whether the number of lashes was limited to 39, in accordance with Jewish law. The Roman soldiers, amused that this weakened man had claimed to be a king, began to mock Him by placing a robe on His shoulders, a crown of thorns on His head, and a wooden staff as a scepter in His right hand. Next, they spat on Jesus and struck Him on the head with the wooden staff. Moreover, when the soldiers tore the robe from Jesus's back, they probably reopened the scourging wounds.

The severe scourging, with its intense pain and appreciable blood loss, probably left Jesus in a pre-shock state. Moreover, hematidrosis had rendered his skin particularly tender. The physical and mental abuse meted out by the Jews and the Romans, as well as the lack of food, water, and sleep, contributed to his generally weakened state. Therefore, even before the actual crucifixion, Jesus's physical condition was at least serious and possibly critical.[44]

Conclusion: Although much more can be said here, I have chosen to provide only a few compelling reasons to believe that it is absolutely impossible for Jesus to have survived the brutal treatment He received at the cross, even with an attempt of resuscitation. Paul, before his conversion, was a persecutor, a mocker, and an enemy of Christians and the Church of Jesus Christ, but, when He found the truth, He made very valid arguments regarding the resurrection of Jesus Christ. His famous account is in 1 Corinthians 15:3-8, where he testifies that Jesus died, was buried, and rose again.

Endnotes

43 "Scourging" http://the-crucifixion.org/scourging.htm#25, (accessed July 1, 2014).

44 To see the full list of references and resources regarding Christ's crucifixion, please see References and Resources section under Biographics

Chapter 21
The Second Coming of Jesus the Messiah

The Christian claim about Jesus is only true because it did indeed take place and there is not a power in this world that can change the historical story of Jesus' existence, birth, ministry, death and resurrection. However, when it comes to Christian theology and practice, there is room for interpretation and understanding. These variations do not weaken Christianity; they merely diversify it. Regardless of interpretation, fundamentally, if one denies the fundamental doctrines of Christianity he or she cannot be a Christian.

Second Coming: The fundamental belief of Christianity is that Jesus will come back again. This belief is as old as Christianity itself, and as a matter of fact, the book of Isaiah in the Old Testament and the Jewish Scriptures in general contain prophecies about the first and second coming of Jesus Christ. Muslims unanimously believe in the second coming of Jesus Christ, and many other Christian and non-Christian faiths believe in the second coming. James writes:

> *Since this Kingdom wasn't established at the First Coming of Christ, it must be established at the Second Coming. God knew that the Jews would reject His Son; so He predetermined that Christ's bloodshed on Calvary would serve as an atonement for the sin of the*

world. This was God's plan all along, to come into the world and pay for the sins of all men (John. 1:29; Rev. 13:8). So the First Coming was one of suffering and shame, but the Second Coming will be one of glory, honor, and praise (1 Pet. 1:10-12). The first time Jesus received a crown of thorns, but when He comes again He will have many crowns (Rev. 19:12). He was the "lamb of God" when He came the first time, but He will be the "lion of the tribe of Judah" the second time (Rev. 5:5). The First Coming gave Jesus Christ to the world, but the Second Coming will give the world to Jesus Christ! Just as David was chosen to be the king of Israel many years before he actually received the kingdom (1 Sam. 16), the Lord Jesus Christ has been chosen to take over the kingdoms of this world and rule as God's "King of Kings" (Rev. 11:15; 19:16).[45]

Regardless of what any other belief system bases their hopes upon, Christians base their hope on the promises of Jesus Christ found in the Scriptures.

Jesus Promised: Jesus made a very clear promise about His second coming. When people asked him questions on various topics, he was sometimes straight forward, other times very vague. When asked about the end times, although He did not give any particular time (Matthew 24:36), He did warn His disciples to look out for certain signs of the second coming of Christ. Jesus said:

Let not your heart be troubled. You are trusting God, now trust in Me. There are many homes up there where my Father lives, and I am going to prepare them for your coming. When everything is ready, then I will come and get you, so that you can always be with Me

where I am. If this weren't so, I would tell you plainly.
And you know where I am going and how to get there.
(John 14:1-3, TLB)

Jesus told His disciples that His second coming would be unexpected and dramatic. "But the day of the Lord will come as a thief in the night, in which the heavens will pass away with a great noise, and the elements will melt with fervent heat; both the earth and the works that are in it will be burned up." (2 Peter 3:10, NKJV) "He who testifies to these things says, "Surely I am coming quickly." Amen. "Even so, come, Lord Jesus." (Revelation 22:20, NKJV)

Angels Promised: There are many denominations, sects, and even heretic churches that do not believe in the second coming of Jesus Christ. However, the Bible teaches us that Jesus's second coming will be literal and real. Not only did Jesus promise this, but His Angels also promised and testified to it.

It was not long afterwards that He rose into the sky and
disappeared into a cloud, leaving them staring after
Him. As they were straining their eyes for another
glimpse, suddenly two white-robed men were standing
there among them, and said, 'Men of Galilee, why are
you standing here staring at the sky? Jesus has gone
away to heaven, and some day, just as He went, He
will return! (Acts 1:10-11, TLB)

Jesus' Second Coming Would Not Be An Isolated Event:
In Jesus' first coming, not many people knew His identity as Christ. Even His own brothers and sisters did not know that He was the Messiah until His death and resurrection. In the Gospel of John 7:1-5, we find the following:

After this, Jesus went around in Galilee. He did not want to go about in Judea because the Jewish leaders there were looking for a way to kill him. But when the Jewish Festival of Tabernacles was near, Jesus' brothers said to him, "Leave Galilee and go to Judea, so that your disciples there may see the works you do. No one who wants to become a public figure acts in secret. Since you are doing these things, show yourself to the world." For even his own brothers did not believe in him (NIV).

In other accounts, we find that His countrymen, neighbors, and relatives did not believe Him (Mark 6:1-6); they tried to kill Him when He told them that He was the Messiah to come (Luke 4:23-30). However, upon His second coming, there will not be any objection because everyone will see Him, "Look, He is coming with the clouds, and every eye will see Him, even those who pierced Him; and all the peoples of the earth will mourn because of Him" (Revelation 1:7, NIV).

No one will need to look for Him, because everyone will able to see Him throughout the world. "For as the lightning comes from the east and flashes to the west, so will be the coming of the Son of Man" (Matthew 24:27, NIV). This is precisely why Jesus warned His disciples, "At that time if anyone says to you, 'Look, here is the Christ!' or 'There He is!' do not believe it. For false Christ's and false prophets will appear and perform great signs and miracles to deceive even the elect—if that were possible. See, I have told you ahead of time. So if anyone tells you, "There He is, out in the desert," do not go out; or, "Here He is, in the inner rooms, do not believe it" (Matthew 24:23-26, NIV).

He Will Come With Great Power And Glory: At the first coming, Jesus was born in a manger, but when He comes the second time He will come as a warrior. The Bible says He will ride from the clouds with glory. "At that time they will see the Son of Man coming in a cloud with power and great glory" (Luke 21:27, NIV).

It will not be a silent night this time. Finally, every knee will bow before Jesus in heaven and on earth and under the earth (Philippians 2:10). "For the Lord himself will come down from heaven, with a loud command, with the voice of the archangel and with the trumpet call of God, and the dead in Christ will rise first. After that, we who are still alive and are left will be caught up with them in the clouds to meet the Lord in the air. And so we will be with the Lord forever" (1 Thessalonians 4:16-17, NIV).

The Bible clearly states the purpose of Jesus's second coming: So also Christ died only once as an offering for the sins of many people; and He will come again, but not to deal again with our sins. This time He will come bringing salvation to all those who are eagerly and patiently waiting for Him (Hebrews 9:28, TLB).

It is this second coming of the Messiah that Christians have hoped for throughout the centuries and died for in that hope. Then we will fully experience the reality of our salvation.

Now you have every grace and blessing; every spiritual gift and power for doing His will are yours during this time of waiting for the return of our Lord Jesus Christ. And He guarantees right up to the end that you will be counted free from all sin and guilt on that day when He returns (1 Corinthians 1:7-8, TLB).

Endnotes

45 James L Melton, copyright 1995, tract: The Second Coming of Jesus Christ.

Part Five
The Validity of the Bible

Chapter 22
Uniqueness of the Bible Among Other Books

There are many good books in the world that teach an immense amount of ethical and moral values, yet they do not claim to be divine. There are also a few books that do claim to be divine. Christians believe and claim that the Bible is a unique book because it is the true revelation of God, and other faiths believe the same about their religious books. Hence, then, the question is: What makes the Bible unique and what makes it stand out amongst all of the rest of the religious books in the world. The answer is very simple. While all of the other books fail to provide evidence that can support their claims, the Bible stands the most difficult tests of authenticity and originality. All of the religious books are respected by their adherents; however, the Bible is even respected by its critics because it invites investigation. There is internal and external evidence to prove that the Bible is truly the word of God. The internal evidence is the text of the Bible that testifies that it is a divine book, and the external evidence indicates that the Bible is truly the supernatural revelation. Revelation means what is revealed, and, in the case of the Bible, God decided to reveal something that is so extraordinary that humans cannot even fully comprehend it. This uniqueness makes the Bible the only truly divine book in the world.

The Unity of the Bible: The Bible is a collection of sixty-six individual books that were written over a period of approximately 1,500 years by 40 different authors in three different languages and on three different continents. Nevertheless, the message is cohesive. As the story unfolds, although most of the men who wrote the books had never met, they hardly could have written so cohesively if they had been sitting in a room together and collaborating on each book.

The Most Scrutinized Book: If you look at the holy books of other religions, you will find that not only have their books hardly been scrutinized, but it seems that there is no one willing or even able to know where to begin to question the validity. Any attempt to investigate the claims that these books make or to question the founders is considered insulting and intolerant. Some of these religions can go as far as taking the life of someone who dares to question them. Therefore, whether it is out of fear or out of respect for the followers of other religions, no other holy book of any major religion (either by the followers of these religions or by non-believers of such religions) has been dissected and brought under scrutiny to test the weight of its stories and claim as much as the Bible. The Bible is the only book that has been scrutinized by philosophers, scientists, archeologists, historians, spiritualists, and the members of believing and non-believing communities.

The idea is very simple. If the author of the Bible is God Himself (if it is a divine revelation), then no matter how many times and who and where it is brought to be tested, it will always stand true. God will defend His word, and no man needs to fight God's fight. In postmodern thinking, instead of asking a simple question, "What is truth?" the easy way out is to discredit the truth, reasoning and the inerrancy of the Bible. It is said over and over again that nothing is truth, or there is truth (if there is), but we cannot really know it. Everything has been swept under the rug in the name of relativism. We have grown accustomed to lying and being lied to, and it seems to me that many of us are comfortable with false assessments and results as long as they do not hurt us. This is the same treatment that the word of God is receiving by irresponsible advocates of postmodernism who claim that the Bible contains errors, and, thus, the case is closed without even launching a thorough investigation.

Geisler and Howe protest and write, "The doctrine of biblical inerrancy is an extremely important one because the truth does matter. This issue reflects on the character of God and is foundational to our understanding of everything the Bible teaches."[46] They give six reasons that might seem very Christian, but they must be considered to understand the internal and external evidences about the truthfulness, inerrancy, and exclusiveness of the Bible. Here are the reasons they present:

1. The Bible itself claims to be perfect.
2. The Bible stands or falls as a whole.
3. The Bible is a reflection of its Author.
4. The Bible judges us, not vice versa.
5. The Bible's message must be taken as a whole.
6. The Bible is our only rule for faith and practice.

They conclude their argument by placing a disclaimer that this does not mean that one who is a follower must blindly believe whatever the Bible says. God invites us to test Him, and His divine Word is the path and revelation to know Him. They write:

> *None of what we have presented here should be taken as a rejection of true scholarship. Biblical inerrancy does not mean that we are to stop using our minds or to accept what the Bible says blindly. We are commanded to study the Word (2 Timothy 2:15), and those who*

search it out are commended (Acts 17:11). Also, we recognize that there are difficult passages in the Bible, as well as sincere disagreements over its interpretation. Our goal is to approach Scripture reverently and prayerfully, and, when we find something we do not understand, we pray harder, study more, and—if the answer still eludes us—humbly acknowledge our own limitations in the face of the perfect Word of God.

It is the fundamental understanding of Christians that the fact that God gave us the Bible is evidence of His love towards humankind. He personally invites us to search for Him, and there are things that we could not have known had God not divinely revealed them to us in the Bible. Now the challenge is this: if it is proven that the Bible is truly the Word of God, then it should be accepted as the final authority for all matters of faith, religious practices, and morals.

Endnotes

46 "What happens after death?" Got Questions Ministries, http://www.gotquestions. org/Biblical-inerrancy.html (accessed July 9, 2014).

Chapter 23
The Authenticity of the Bible

There is a lot of evidence that authenticates the Bible, and it is crucial to look into this evidence with an unbiased mind. Sometimes, it is our biased opinion that keeps us away from the truth. A fair examination of the following evidence can certainly challenge a skeptic.

Internal Evidences: As stated earlier, the unity of the all sixty-six individual books of the Bible is unique from all other books (both holy and unholy) and is evidence of the divine origin of the Bible, which God inspired men to record.

1. **Testimonies of the human authors**. There are two types of testimonies we find in the human authorship of the Bible.

    Type one: They testified about each other. There are numerous passages in the Bible where one human author testifies about the others, describing how God spoke through him. Thus, the revelation continues to unfold from one chosen man to another.

    Type two: They testified about God's divine authorship. Paul testifies to the divine inspiration of the Bible in these words "… from infancy you have known the holy Scriptures, which are able to make you wise for salvation through faith in Christ Jesus. All Scripture is God-breathed and is useful for teaching, rebuking, correcting and training in righteousness, so that the man of God may be thoroughly equipped for every good work." (2 Timothy 3:15-17)

2. **Prophecies**. There are hundreds of detailed prophecies in the Bible relating to the future of individual nations, cities, people groups, and especially about the nation of Israel. There are also many prophecies concerning the coming of the Messiah, the Savior of all who would believe in Him. Complementing the unity of the Bible, all of the events and prophecies point towards the need for and the coming of the Messiah. Unlike the prophecies found in other religious books, biblical prophecies are extremely detailed. There are over three hundred prophecies concerning Jesus Christ in the Old Testament. The book of Daniel is a prime example. There are 2,500 years of accurate historical fulfillment so far in this prophecy.

3. **Miraculous power**. A powerful testimony of the divine origin of the Bible can be seen in the miraculous changes that take place in the lives of those who read it. Each individual who has read it can testify to the unique authority and power that the Bible has. In times of pain, sorrow, and hopelessness, it has brought new hope and joy. While this piece of evidence is more subjective than the others, it is no less meaningful and tangible. Even today, scholars use qualitative methods to conduct reliable research to record certain phenomena. The idea is to collect the experiences of people and draw a conclusion. For example, there are reports of confessions of drug addicts who have been cured, broken relationships that have been mended, hardened criminals reformed, depressed, transformed, and enemies reconciled through the power of the Bible. The Bible's authority is unlike any other book

ever written. This authority and power is best seen in the way that countless lives have been transformed by the supernatural power of God's Word. The Bible possesses a dynamic and transforming power that is only possible because it is truly God's Word.

External Evidences: There is also external evidence that indicates that the Bible is truly the Word of God.

1. **Historicity**. The first is the historicity of the Bible. Because the Bible details historical events, its truthfulness and accuracy are subject to verification like any other historical document. Through both archaeological evidence and other writings, the historical accounts of the Bible have been proven time and time again to be accurate and true. In fact, all of the archaeological and manuscript evidence supporting the Bible makes it the best documented book from the ancient world. The fact that the Bible accurately and truthfully records historically verifiable events is a great indication of its truthfulness and helps substantiate its claim to be the very Word of God.

2. **The Integrity of the human authors**. Another piece of external evidence that the Bible is truly God's Word is the integrity of its human authors. As mentioned earlier, God used men from many walks of life to record His words. In studying the lives of these men, we find them to be honest and sincere. The fact that they were willing to die often excruciating deaths for what they believed testifies that these ordinary yet honest men truly believed what God had spoken to them. The men who wrote the New Testament and many hundreds of other believers (1 Corinthians 15:6) knew the truth of their message because they had seen and spent time with Jesus Christ after He had risen

from the dead. Seeing the risen Christ had a tremendous impact on them. They went from hiding in fear to being willing to die for the message God had revealed to them.

3. **Indestructibility**. A final piece of external evidence is the indestructibility of the Bible. Because of its importance and its claim to be the very Word of God, the Bible has suffered more vicious attacks and attempts to destroy it than any other book in history. From early Roman Emperors like Diocletian, to communist dictators and to modern-day atheists and agnostics, the Bible has withstood and outlasted all of its attackers and is still today the most widely published book in the world.

Throughout time, skeptics have regarded the Bible as mythological, but archeology has confirmed it as historical. Opponents have attacked its teaching as primitive and outdated, but its moral and legal concepts and teachings have had a positive influence on societies and cultures throughout the world. It continues to be attacked by pseudo-science, psychology, and political movements, yet it remains just as true and relevant today as it was when it was first written. It is a book that has transformed countless lives and cultures throughout the last 2,000 years. No matter how its opponents try to attack, destroy, or discredit it, the Bible remains, and its veracity and impact on lives is unmistakable. The accuracy has been preserved despite every attempt to corrupt, attack, or destroy it, the Bible is truly God's Word and is supernaturally protected by Him. It should not surprise us that, no matter how the Bible is attacked, it always comes out unchanged and unscathed. After all, Jesus said, "Heaven and earth will pass away, but my words will never pass away" (Mark 13:31). After looking at this evidence, one can say without a doubt that, yes, the Bible is truly God's Word.

Part Six
The Issue of Pain and Suffering

Chapter 24
Why God Allows Suffering

The Bible teaches us that God is loving and all powerful. He can do whatever He wants. There is no one in the known or unknown world who can challenge His authority. Daniel says "All the peoples of the earth are regarded as nothing. He does as He pleases with the powers of heaven and the peoples of the earth. No one can hold back his hand or say to him: "What have you done?" (Daniel 4:35 NIV) "He is before all things, and in him all things hold together" (Col. 1:17 NIV). When it comes to our faith and suffering, different people react differently, and perhaps this is because suffering affects us differently. Generally speaking, there are two types and at least four major sources of suffering. Nonetheless, God in His sovereignty alone is capable to remove, inflict, block, or allow this pain. Therefore, when dealing with suffering, people cannot avoid blaming God, whether they pronounce faith in Him or not.

Time issue of April 8, 1966 published a piece by Friedrich Nietzsche on the subject of "Is God Dead?" He reflects on the cultural shift from faith to rationalism and science through an allegorical story of a man who is looking for God but can't find Him. In a form of questions Nietzsche sums up the deepest flaws of our culture that even though we despise God because of our self-centeredness and self-pride yet we desire to be exalted to the position of gods. He writes,

"Where has God gone?" he cried. "I shall tell you. We have killed him—you and I. We are his murderers. But how have we done this? How were we able to drink up the sea? Who gave us the sponge to wipe away the entire horizon? What did we do when we unchained the earth from its sun? Whither is it moving now? Whither are we moving now? Away from all suns? Are we not perpetually falling? Backward, sideward, forward, in all directions? Is there any up or down left? Are we not straying as through an infinite nothing? Do we not feel the breath of empty space? Has it not become colder? Is it not more and more night coming on all the time? Must not lanterns be lit in the morning? Do we not hear anything yet of the noise of the gravediggers who are burying God? Do we not smell anything yet of God's decomposition? Gods too decompose. God is dead. God remains dead. And we have killed him. How shall we, murderers of all murderers, console ourselves? That which was the holiest and mightiest of all that the world has yet possessed has bled to death under our knives. Who will wipe this blood off us? With what water could we purify ourselves? What festivals of atonement, what sacred games shall we need to invent? Is not the greatness of this deed too great for us? Must we not ourselves become gods simply to be worthy of it? There has never been a greater deed; and whosoever shall be born after us—for the sake of this deed he shall be part of a higher history than all history hitherto."[47]

Our generation is the first to realize that the argument of the existence of God begins with the death of God, and the perpetrator is none other than our culture and skepticism. It has done away with the guilt that has kept man within the boundaries of moral, social, and spiritual values. Setting man free from such values means making him inhuman. By taking a closer look at our bloodless, self-centered, and guilt-free society that has declared religion to be nothing more than superstitions and God to be a mere weak expression of human dignity—only a figment of one's imagination—we can conclude that the dangerous path we have adopted has set us up for self-destruction. It is this guilt-free, Godless, and self-centered, mentality that makes a mere man think that he is an invincible god on earth, and he, therefore, does what he deems fit to control and maintain his power. Of such a mentality are Joseph Vissarionovich Stalin, who brought about the death of more than 20 million of his own people while holding the Soviet Union in an iron grip for 29 years,[48] and Adolf Hitler, whose policies of territorial conquest and racial subjugation brought about the death and destruction to tens of millions of people, including the genocide of some six million Jews in what is now known as the Holocaust.[49] These are only two examples out of many.

Type One Suffering: Type one suffering is a part of every human's experience. It is general suffering, where pain, illness, and death produce grievances and sorrow. The natural process of life, from birth to death, carries many incidents of suffering. Natural disasters are also part of type one suffering—floods, famines, earthquakes, and even volcanic eruptions. This suffering also includes human brutality, resulting in eradication of certain ethnic people groups, poverty, hunger, lack of basic human needs, and lack of freedom of speech and expression. All of these create human suffering. Nietzsche said, "What really raises one's indignation against suffering is not the suffering intrinsically, but the senselessness of suffering."[50] It has been said that pain and suffering are inevitable, but misery is optional.

Besides, if we talk about the good news and always are happy and joyful, how would we really know that there is bad news, that there is unhappiness, sorrow, and suffering? Despite our own understanding of suffering and the reasons behind it, the bigger purpose behind suffering (which is not limited to an individual's personal opinion) determines the true understanding of human existence and answers the most commonly asked question: "What is the purpose of my life?" This purpose will not be accomplished without our perspective on the problem of pain. Suffering helps humanity unite for a single purpose; it removes our petty differences and invites us to work together.

Type Two Suffering: Type two suffering is a very specific kind of suffering, targeted towards a specific people group, and is certainly a part of the divine plan. In this type, evil wins, the violent force prospers and injustice triumphs. This is the suffering that is prescribed by the divine to let injustice, evil and darkness win for a brief period of time before they are put an end to forever. Even in this, God remains just. This type includes people who believe in God. Here are a few reasons why type two is God's plan for those who seek to follow Him:

- **Reason No. 1**. When things are going well, we are okay with God. We must be okay with God when things are not going well for us.

- **Reason No. 2**. When you strip away all of those gifts and blessings, then the real you will come out. e.g; Job. Either you will solely trust in God, or you will curse God. No longer lukewarm, you will be tested and proven to be hot or cold. Unfortunately, many theists, including Christians, are lukewarm.

- **Reason No. 3**. When trials arise, our church lives and our prayer lives become very serious. Do not wait for trials to get serious with God; we must follow with our whole beings and remain constantly in the presence of God.

■ **Reason No. 4.** So that we may learn although God is always able to deliver us from pain and suffering, whether it is from His hand or not, He always acts according to His good and perfect will. In Jeremiah 32:26-27 God said, "I am the Lord, the God of all mankind. Is anything too hard for me?" (NIV).

Job's miseries and the maturity that Job expressed was the outcome of deep trust in God and God's deep trust in the faithfulness of Job. Is it not interesting that God has faith in us that we will remain faithful to Him, no matter what? The example that Job set is a model for every believer. No matter who causes the suffering, our God is always in control. Job would never have learned what he learned without going through pain and suffering. He did not know whether he would come out alive from his misery; he even desired death. But when God moved with His might, not only was Job's health, wealth, and prestige restored, it was doubled.

> *Ah, Sovereign Lord, you have made the heavens and the earth by your great power and outstretched arm. Nothing is too hard for you. You show love to thousands but bring the punishment for the parents' sins into the laps of their children after them. Great and mighty God, whose name is the Lord Almighty, great are your purposes and mighty are your deeds. Your eyes are open to the ways of all mankind; you reward each person according to their conduct and as their deeds deserve (Jeremiah 32:17-19, NIV).*

To remind us who is in charge, He shakes us to let us know not to get too comfortable with this world because it is a temporary place, and our days on this earth, no matter how long or painful, are still nothing compared to eternity. We must remember:

1. God not only comforts the inflicted, but sometimes He inflicts the comfortable.

2. God always has His reasons. He brings good news and he brings adversities, to prove us true to our faith.

3. God is not as interested in our happiness as He is in our holiness.

False theologies of health, wealth, and prosperity proclaim that, if you are not good with God, you will suffer, and if you did something wrong you will suffer. (To understand more, see Ch.11 under "False Theology.")

Endnotes

47 Friedrich Nietzsche "Is God Dead" Time. April 08, 1966. http://content.time. com/time/magazine/article/0,9171,835309,00.html, (accessed, July 1, 2014).

48 Wonderslist, "10 Most Cruel Rulers Ever in History" http://www.wonderslist. com/10-most-cruel-rulers-ever-in-history/, (accessed, July 1, 2014).

49 Ibid.

50 Nietzche, "Philosphy of suffering" http://www.angelfire.com/ut/inorbit/Quotes-Suffering.html, (accessed June 30, 2014).

Chapter 25
Humans are the Instruments of Their Own Suffering

I assure you that, no matter what the source of your suffering is, God is mighty to save; Psalm 34:19 says "The righteous person may have many troubles, but the LORD delivers him from them all;" Notice, it does not say that it delivers from one or two, but from all of them, and He does so regardless of the source of those troubles. Also, the promise is not for the unrighteous, it is an exclusive statement for the righteous only, determined by God and not by man because God is the one who knows the deepest desires of our hearts. Psalm 11:5, however, warns us that "the wicked, those who love violence, He hates with a passion."

God's Passion is part of His holiness. Many times we confuse God's holiness with His righteousness. We think God's holiness means God is good. While it is true that He is good, let us not mistake this for His being Holy. His holiness means that He is perfect, and there is no other like Him whatsoever, not even one. Subsequently, in terms of His holiness, if I ask, "Who is more like God? Is it the angel Gabriel, or the young man who shot so many innocent children in Connecticut?" You may answer "of course Gabriel," the answer is "Neither," because no one is like God in His holiness. Therefore, when Psalm 11:5 uses the phrase "He (God) hates with a passion," it means a kind of passion and a kind of hate that no one can exercise other than God Himself.

It was God's passion that killed all of the men, women, and animals in Noah's days because He hated the wickedness He saw; it was also by His passion of love that He delivered Noah, his family, and the animals from the flood. It was His passion that burned Sodom and Gomorrah to the ground because He hated the wickedness of their hearts, but it was also by His passion of love that He took Himself to the cross to deliver us all as a perfect sacrifice. Thus, the Bible testifies, "and these whom He predestined, He also called; and these whom He called, He also justified; and these whom He justified, He also glorified" (Roman 8:30 NIV). Proverbs 24:16 says, "For a righteous man falls seven times, and rises again, But the wicked stumble in time of calamity" (NASB).

The righteous and the wicked alike fall prey to their own choices and decisions that invite infliction upon them. Sometimes suffering comes from our own hands because every action has a reaction. The consequences of our actions can bring misery and pain.

In 2010, I was in the middle of defending my doctorate dissertation. I remember my professor and the chair of my dissertation committee telling me "Do not stop working on your dissertation because Satan is going to strike you over and over again. You may even lose a loved one." It was not long after that when I received news that a drunk driver ran through a red light and crushed the car of the speaker of those very prophetic words, killing her and her son. The man was drunk and the consequence was the death of two innocent people, and his arrest. "Do not be deceived: God is not mocked, for whatever one sows, that will he also reap." Galatians 6:7 (ESV).

This means that if you sow righteousness, you will reap righteousness, and if you sow wickedness, you will reap wickedness.

Drinking and driving is a crime, and if a drunk driver commits this crime that leads to an accident, as he faces criminal charges he cannot blame anyone but himself. He sowed the wickedness and is reaping the return of wickedness in jail. However, I continue to grieve over the death of my professor and her son. They did not do anything wrong, yet they became the victims of someone else's wrong doing. Even though throughout her whole life she sowed righteousness, she died at such a young age, along with her son. However, she knew that this world is temporary and that soon she would be home in heaven.

Fruit of Deception: Half of the Christian world has become slaves to righteous deeds to gain access to God minimizing the value of the perfect atonement of Christ and the other half has totally forgotten the significance of living a holy and righteous life so that the work of God through Christ may be fully manifested in us and through us. If you think you are holier and more righteous than others, you have already sowed a seed of pride and have set yourself up for more temptation. This is deceiving yourself and mocking God.

Job warns us in "Would it turn out well if he (God) examined you? Could you deceive him as you might deceive a mortal?" (Job. 13:9 NIV). The point is this, you may fool others, even yourself into believing that you are not wicked, but, before God, there is no one who is righteous.

You may look at a person and say "Indeed, this person does not deserve such pain and suffering" or vise versa. This is nothing more than the fruit of deception that you are witnessing. Recently, I have been exposed to such deception in a very real way. It was a two-fold deception. Many of you probably remember the week when the U.S. Supreme Court heard two gay marriage cases. There had been a huge campaign on the

Internet to gain support for the movement and to push the U. S Supreme Court to make a decision in favor of the gay community. The questions were phrased in very deceptive ways, such as, "Do you support equality in marriage?" or "Do you support love?" Perhaps some people said "yes" to these things because they thought that they referred to love or equality overall, with no agenda towards either side; the actual meaning was often hidden. It was actually meant to signify support of the equal rights of a man to marry a man and a woman to marry a woman.

Another very important case is in process now regarding the definition of life in the womb. It is about rights. People are standing for rights, just like those who stand for the rights of a gay man or a gay woman—they stand for abortion. They do not give the right to a living being to speak simply because the person is not born yet. John Piper said, "Christ died that we might live. This is the opposite of abortion. Abortion kills that someone might live differently."

"But you have planted wickedness, you have reaped evil, you have eaten the fruit of deception." Hosea 10:13 (NIV).

We are being deceived by each other. There are those who raise their voice for the right to do evil, yet there is no such voice for justice. There are many issues that society encourages and considers harmless, yet God condemns them categorically. They all come from our evil desires and are the fruit of deception. "Do you not know that wrongdoers will not inherit the kingdom of God? Do not be deceived: Neither the sexually immoral nor idolaters nor adulterers nor men who have sex with men." 1 Corinthians 6:9 (NIV). Here are a few reasons why we are the way that we are.

Reason no. 1. The Bible teaches that, since the fall of Adam, our souls have been broken. Sin has altered our way of thinking.

We carry a corrupt nature that encourages us to do evil. This means that even when we are indulging in evil work, we do not feel that we are a part of that evil. Injustice is not only when one does evil, but it is when one also does not speak up against injustice knowingly being done. Ecclesiastes 5:8 says, "If you see in a province the oppression of the poor and the violation of justice and righteousness, do not be amazed at the matter, for the high official is watched by a higher one, and there are yet higher ones over them" (ESV). Yet we do nothing to stop an oppressor.

Micah 6:8 says, "He has told you, O man, what is good; and what does the Lord require of you but to do justice, and to love kindness, and to walk humbly with your God?" (ESV). Unfortunately, today we are in a society that is trying to choke moral values, ethics, God, and the recognition of right and wrong to death. When one raises the question of right and wrong, he suffocates the proponents of relativism where there is no right and wrong resulting into social suicide. We raise the question, "Why does God allow suffering?" Yet we do not acknowledge that we are also the source of suffering because we neither do good nor justice. Love and kindness are the words of the Bible being redefined in social circles to gain control, self-pleasure, and satisfaction of sinful lusts and cravings, subsequently turning this world into one big brothel.

Reason no. 2. Our decisions and choices have had and continue to have an effect on the world that we live in; consequently, this world is broken and causes pain and suffering to its inhabitants. We play a big role in mobilizing God's passion to hate or love us. We bring calamity upon ourselves by running our lives the way we please (Psalm 11:5 ESV). If I drive too fast, run a red light, or take a U-turn where it is clearly marked not to, the inevitability of an accident is given.

How about abusing our bodies? Much of our suffering is a direct result of the life we choose to lead. When one ignores the written warning on cigarettes and faces the consequences later, or eats too much and becomes overweight and increases their risk of heart disease and diabetes, who is there to blame?

Reason no. 3. Although we are made in the image of God, we have lost our purity. The absence of the glue that holds us and this universe together makes us broken people.

The Son is the image of the invisible God, the firstborn over all creation. For in him all things were created: things in heaven and on earth, visible and invisible, whether thrones or powers or rulers or authorities; all things have been created through him and for him. He is before all things, and in him all things hold together. And he is the head of the body, the church; he is the beginning and the firstborn from among the dead, so that in everything he might have the supremacy. For God was pleased to have all his fullness dwell in him, and through him to reconcile to himself all things, whether things on earth or things in heaven, by making peace through his blood, shed on the cross (Colossians 1:15-20 NIV).

Not only are we broken people resulting in broken families, broken marriages, and broken homes, but also the universe is broken and cries for restoration.

Chapter 26
This World is the Instrument of Our Suffering

Every day, horrific things are taking place. We have heard rumors of war here in America. North Korea is talking about destroying South Korea and the United States, and Iran has renewed its vow to annihilate Israel and continue its nuclear program. Elsewhere, human rights have been totally ignored. Thousands of people have been killed or thrown into jails by oppressors, and the voice of justice has been sucked out of the justice system in order to maintain control over the people.

At home, in the wake of the Boston Marathon bombing in 2013, we are again reminded of our vulnerability. It is inconceivable to us that we, as the super power of the world, were unable to uncover the culprits or the motive behind this attack for quite some time.

The evidence of suffering, pain, evil, and death are scattered all over the globe, and, in the midst of all of this, even with our best technological advancements, we find ourselves utterly helpless. From the ashes of such suffering and pain, evil and death weaken us in our spirits but strengthen us in anger to raise the question of "Why does God allow suffering?"

In Matthew 7:13-29, Jesus gives an example of four items, discussing and emphasizing two lifestyles, two people groups, and two types of worlds. Each item is a comparison.

"The Narrow and Wide Gates" (verses 13-14) compares the majority and the minority, good choices and bad choices, good decisions and bad decisions, visible and the invisible. "True and False Prophets" (verses 15:20) compares the true and false teachers of the Word. "True and False Disciples" (verses 21-23) compares committed Christians and worldly Christians. "The Wise and Foolish Builders" (verses 24-27) compares the hearers and the doers of the Word.

Each and every one of these comparisons is a clear teaching about two choices that you and I make. Christ paints a beautiful yet simple picture to show us that this world is in conflict with the world that God desires. He tells us that to the naked eye, it appears that all is well, healthy, and magnificent—yet it is a dying world. He tells us that whoever chooses to follow the ways of this world chooses death, pain, suffering, and sorrow for him or herself. This world is destined to be destroyed and renewed. The evil in this world has eaten it up from the inside out and left it hollow. Just one more blow and what we see today will cease to exist. Like bone cancer, human decisions and choices that defile God and reject His grace, mercy, and compassion are infecting every organism of our society. Therefore, there are many who enter through the wide gate—even Christians who hope under false precepts that it will take them to eternal life.

This is why Jesus told us that we will be taught, preached, and lied to by false prophets. False teachers will tell us that everything is well, that God wants you to be happy, rich, healthy, and that all suffering and poverty is from Satan. We will even hear that Hell does not exist, because why would a good God send people to Hell? We will be told that things are getting better, people are good naturally, there is good in you regardless of whether you follow Christ or not, and there are many ways to get to God, so let us not make exclusive claims about Christ. The Bible says, "But the day of the Lord will come like a thief, in which the heavens will pass away with a roar and the elements will be destroyed with intense heat, and the earth and its works will be burned up" (2 Peter 3:10 NASB).

This idea of doing works to gain salvation, which is prominent in Judaism, Buddhism, Hinduism, Islam and even Christianity, is sending more people to Hell than brothels ever have. Christianity is more than a notion of morality; it is more than some set of laws and principles. It is about a revolution in our character. When one embraces Christianity—or rather, when Christianity embraces someone- it revolutionizes his or her inner being. The core being of a person transforms into a renewed being, reflecting the radical lifestyle that Jesus demonstrated in His earthly ministry. Therefore, a true Christian (follower of Christ) does not work to gain salvation, but his works are the result of his salvation. When we are truly transformed, we begin to understand that sometimes suffering comes from the hands of this world; here are three reasons why:

- ■ **Reason no. 1**. The world is broken and seeks restoration.
- ■ **Reason no. 2**. The earth is full with wickedness and seeks revenge.
- ■ **Reason no. 3**. The earth is cursed, and, thus, produces pain and suffering.

Michael McCarthy was, until recently, an environmental editor for 15 years at a well-known U.K based newspaper, the Independent. His credentials speak for him: He is one of Britain's leading writers on the environment and the natural world. He has won numerous awards as a journalist and is a specialist in the field of environmental science and zoology. On Friday, March 29, 2013, right before Easter, McCarthy published his last article for the *Independent* entitled: "Man is fallen and will destroy the Earth—but at least we greens made him wait."[51] He poses two questions:

Are people good? Is humankind basically benign? In our current belief system, which we might term liberal secular humanism, which has held sway in the West since the Second World War, and which promotes human progress and well-being, only one response is permitted: Yes, of course! Any suggestion that there might be something wrong with people as a whole, with Man as a species, is absolute anathema. For if, over the past decade and a half, you have closely observed what is happening to the Earth, week in, week out, you may take a dark view of the future; and I do. The reason is that the Earth is under threat, as it has never been before, from the ever more oppressive scale of the human enterprise: from the activities of a world population which doubled from three to six billion in four short decades, between 1960 and 2000, and which, in the four decades to come, will probably increase by three billion more.

These activities are now wiping out ecosystems and species, across the world, at an ever increasing rate: the forests are chain sawed; the oceans are strip mined of their fish; the rivers, especially in the developing world, are ever more polluted; the farmland is rendered sterile of all but the monoculture crop by demented dosing with pesticides; the farmland insects and wild flowers and many of the birds have gone.

People are doing this. Let's be clear about it. It's not some natural phenomenon, like an earthquake or a volcanic eruption. It's the actions of Homo sapiens. What we are witnessing is a fundamental clash

*between the species, and the planet on which he lives,
which is going to worsen steadily, and the more closely
you observe it—or at least, the more closely I have
observed it, over the past 15 years—the more I have
thought that there is something fundamentally wrong
with Homo sapiens himself. Man seems to be Earth's
problem child. We humans have always thought
ourselves different in kind from other creatures, prin-
cipally for our use of language and our possession
of consciousness, but there is another reason for our
uniqueness, which is becoming ever clearer: we are
the only species capable of destroying our own home.
And it looks like we will.*

Not as a Christian, but purely as a scientist, he continues:

*In the Christian view of the world, Man is fallen,
yet because of Christ's self-sacrifice on the cross on
Good Friday, Man is redeemed. You may think of the
idea of The Fall as simply the story of Adam eating
the forbidden fruit, but such a myth is not of itself
what has gripped some of the most powerful minds
in history (and I believe including McCathy himself).
Rather, the idea of fallen Man gives potent expression
to that prominent part of the human character which
has been observed, down the ages, with horror: our
terrible potential for destruction, for causing suffering
to others and, indeed, now, for destroying our own
home (all of which liberal secular humanism prefers
not to look at). In the Christian worldview, humankind
is not basically benign. People are not good.*

Is it not phenomenal that the Christian message does not end
with the bad news that science and philosophy have to offer, but
with hope? The suffering that this world presents to its inhabi-

tants, biblically, historically, scientifically, and spiritually can be attested to, and the end result will be very simple- that no one has the power to stop it other than God. You see this in Jesus's words in Matthew 5:43-48:

> *You have heard that it was said, 'Love your neighbor and hate your enemy.' But I tell you, love your enemies and pray for those who persecute you, that you may be children of your Father in heaven. He causes his sun to rise on the evil and the good, and sends rain on the righteous and the unrighteous. If you love those who love you, what reward will you get? Are not even the tax collectors doing that? And if you greet only your own people, what are you doing more than others? Do not even pagans do that? Be perfect, therefore, as your heavenly Father is perfect (NIV).*

This will never make sense to this world; this is why the end will come, and destruction will take place. However, God Himself promised the renewing of this earth. Here are three questions that help us to understand God's intentions about this world and the world to come:

1. **Where did He make that promise?** John saw and wrote by the inspiration of the Holy Spirit in Revelation 21:1: "Then I saw a new heaven and a new earth, for the first heaven and the first earth had passed away, and there was no longer any sea" (NIV). It was in accordance with the promise God made long before John's time. In Isaiah 65:17, we find God saying, "See, I will create new heavens and a new earth. The former things will not be remembered, nor will they come to mind" (NIV). God promises not only new heavens and earth, but also that you will not even remember the old things, the pain and

the suffering you have gone through. In Isaiah 60:21 God says, "Then all your people will be righteous and they will possess the land forever. They are the shoot I have planted, the work of my hands, for the display of my splendor" (NIV). For His own glory and majesty God will fulfill His promise.

Christians should be the embodiment of the hope we have in Christ. 2 Peter 3:13 says, "But according to his promise we are waiting for new heavens and a new earth in which righteousness dwells" (ESV); Peter goes on to tell us that His promises are true, but you must leave the old ways of your life, start living righteously now, and suffer for a little longer. "Through these he has given us his very great and precious promises, so that through them you may participate in the divine nature, having escaped the corruption in the world caused by evil desires" (2 Peter 1:4 NIV).

The Bible says that God will bring forth a new heaven and earth for the display of His splendor, and there will no more pain or sorrow, hate or crime, death or war, only peace. "The wolf and the lamb will feed together, and the lion will eat straw like the ox, and dust will be the serpent's food. They will neither harm nor destroy on all my holy mountain, says the LORD" (Isaiah 65:25 NIV).

2. **Will the new earth and heaven be destroyed ever again?** The answer is "No." Creation itself will be liberated from its bondage to decay and brought into the freedom and glory of the children of God. Romans 8:21

3. **Can sin again enter into the new heaven and earth like the world we live in now?** The answer is "NO." John writes in Revelation 21:27 "Nothing impure will ever

enter it, nor will anyone who does what is shameful or deceitful, but only those whose names are written in the Lamb's book of life."

Endnotes

51 McCarthy Michael, Man is fallen and will destroy the Earth—but at least we greens made him wait, Friday 29 March 2013, The Independent (also available online: http://www.independent.co.uk/voices/comment/man-is-fallen-and-will-destroy-the-earth--but-at-least-we-greens-made-him-wait-8554548.html) (accessed July 1, 2014).

Chapter 27
Satan is the Instrument of Our Suffering

I will spend extra time on this subject because it is imperative to understanding that Satan uses all other sources of our suffering to make sure that we curse God. One evening about 7:15pm I received a text message from a brother in my church. The message read:

> *"Brother and Pastor Javed prayer request please for family, especially, my nephew, his father, and my oldest brother could be passing on at any moment."*

I received the message on my cell phone and immediately knew it was urgent, absolutely more important than anything else I was doing at that moment. The brother who wrote the message is a very articulate man, so such a short and inarticulate message with such disturbing news told me much more than the words alone. Beneath those words, one could excavate a clear sense of urgency, helplessness, grief, sorrow, yet also hope, love, care, and perhaps a miracle. His message did not end there. He completed that short message with a very short but powerful statement that demonstrated this brother's utmost desire to trust in the Lord's sovereign will.

"God's grace is sufficient," he wrote.

Although I suspected that my words would be inadequate to heal his wounds, trusting in the common hope we share in Christ,

I responded: "I am so sorry to hear that; you never mentioned him before. May the Lord and His grace cover you all and bring a peace that is deeper than the sea and higher than the heavens. May His mercy and love comfort you all in this time of sorrow and grief. I am in prayer with you my dear brother."

He responded right away, "Thank you. It has been an ongoing process. However, I was sent the week of Hurricane Sandy to get his confession of Christ. Hallelujah! Amen."

The following evening, about 24 hours later at 7:24 p.m., I received another message from him: "Thank you again. It is well; my brother is with the Lord."

Again, one small statement, "It is well," referring to the hymn "It is well with my soul" was enough to tell me the full story. The words came as a reflection at a time of great personal tragedy from a man whose commitment to the Christ was like that of Job's. The story goes like this:

> *Horatio and his wife Anna were committed supporters and close friends of D.L. Moody, the famous preacher and founder of the Moody Bible Institute. In 1870, hardships attacked their life. The Spaffords' only son was killed by scarlet fever at the age of four. A year later, fire ravaged real estate holdings along the shores of Lake Michigan that Horatio had heavily invested in. In 1871, every one of these holdings was destroyed by the great Chicago Fire.*
>
> *Needing a sabbatical from the stressful toll that these disasters had taken on the family, Horatio decided to take his wife and four daughters on a holiday to England. It would be a time of rest for the family, and it would help D.L. Moody travel around Britain on a great evangelistic campaigns. Horatio and Anna planned to join Moody in late 1873. When*

the time came, the Spaffords traveled to New York in November to catch a ship. Just before they set sail, a last-minute business development caused Horatio to delay. Instead of letting this ruin the family holiday, Horatio persuaded his family to go as planned. He would follow later. Anna and her four daughters sailed East to Europe while Horatio returned West to Chicago. Nine days later, Spafford received a telegram from his wife in Wales. It read: "Saved alone."

On November 2, 1873, the ship that Anna and her four daughters took sank in only 12 minutes, claiming the lives of 226 people, including the four daughters. Anna was only saved by a plank that floated beneath her unconscious body and propped her up.

Upon hearing the terrible news, Horatio boarded the next ship out of New York to join his bereaved wife. When his ship passed the place where his daughters' ship had wrecked, Horatio returned to his cabin and penned the lyrics of his great hymn.[52]

Such understanding of pain and suffering, where one comes to the simple confession and realization that "It is well" and "God's grace is sufficient" in the face of the most devastating situations has become very rare in the church of Jesus Christ. If you are not familiar with the hymn "When peace, like a river, attendeth my way…it is well with my soul," I would encourage you to read the lyrics. of the hymn When it comes to dealing with pain and suffering, it is crucial for Christians to understand the following five principles.

Principle no. 1. God has absolute control over our circumstances, even when Satan is the instrument of destruction and pain. In Job 1:12 God said to Job, "Behold, all that he has is in your power, only do not put forth your hand on him" (NASB). Notice how God did not give him all of the control, it was commanded that Satan must not touch his life. In John Piper's words:

> *Our vision of God in relation to evil and suffering was shown to be frivolous. The church has not been spending its energy to go deep with the unfathomable God of the Bible. Against the overwhelming weight and seriousness of the Bible, much of the church is choosing, at this very moment, to become more light and shallow and entertainment-oriented, and therefore successful in its irrelevance to massive suffering and evil. The popular God of fun-church is simply too small and too affable to hold a hurricane in his hand. The biblical categories of God's sovereignty lie like land mines in the pages of the Bible waiting for someone to seriously open the book. They don't kill, but they do explode trivial notions of the Almighty.*[53]

Thus, the sovereignty of God covers all that is seen and unseen, that which was, is and is to come. I believe that *sometimes we give way too much credit to Satan for things that happen in our lives.* In doing so, we lose sight of what God is trying to accomplish through our suffering. Or we go to the other extreme and blame God for everything, and forget that He is sovereign and the only one who can give us the peace that surpasses human understanding. Although Satan has the power to inflict God's people, he has absolutely no power to put his hand against God's people without God's permission. Therefore, it is not only imperative to understand the sovereignty of God over Satan, but it is also important to understand the limitations that Satan is bound to. Job 1:10 is Satan's acknowledgement of his boundaries and limitations; he cannot and will not ever be able harm what is protected by God. It is interesting what the verse says, "Have you not made a hedge about him and his house and all that he has, on ever side" (NASB) as if Satan went out and scouted the area and tried to break in but was unable to find any unprotected side.

I remember back in early 2000 when my dad received a call from someone in a nearby town. When he went to visit this man, he found him on his deathbed. My dad immediately recognized him as one of the leaders behind his own arrest a few years earlier for building a church. The man addressed my father with much humility and told him that he has been tormented over and over in his dreams. He was given my father's name to call and ask for prayer. My mother and father both prayed for the dying man, asking that the Lord may forgive his sins against them and heal him. To make a long story short, the man also inquired of something that I found very disturbing, yet encouraging. He said there had been times when he led small teams of two or three men to attack and kill my father. He confessed that they never succeeded because my dad and our house were guarded with tall men. He asked who they were. My dad never responded, but we knew that there were no guards. We also knew it was something that only those men could see because God was protecting His people.

Principle no. 2. God has absolute dominion over Satan and his demons. Neither he nor His demons can violate God's sovereign will and plan for us. *Satan is neither eternal nor infinite. All he knows is within the limits of time and space, and he cannot alter or determine the path or the end of our life, unless we give in to our evil desires, or God allows it.* James 1:13-15 says, "When tempted, no one should say, 'God is tempting me.' For God cannot be tempted by evil, nor does he tempt anyone; but each person is tempted when they are dragged away by their own evil desire and enticed. Then, after desire has conceived, it gives birth to sin; and sin, when it is full-grown, gives birth to death" (NIV).

God's desire and plan for us in His sovereignty is very simple. Jesus said, "I am the gate; whoever enters through me will be saved. They will come in and go out, and find pasture. The thief comes only to steal and kill and destroy; I have come that they may have life, and have it to the full" (John 10:9-10 NIV).

Principle no. 3. The dominion Satan enjoys and exercises on this earth is not his own but is extended to him for a specific duration of time.

Matthew 8:29 gives us a glimpse into the timeline of supernatural evil. The demons cry out, "What do you want with us, Son of God?" they shouted. "Have you come here to torture us before the appointed time?" (NIV)—they know a time is set for their final destruction. In Luke 4:5-7, we read, "The devil led him up to a high place and showed him in an instant all the kingdoms of the world. And he said to him, 'I will give you all their authority and splendor; it has been given to me, and I can give it to anyone I want to. If you worship me, it will all be yours' "(NIV). Notice Satan's confession in verse 6: that it has been given to him. Which means we should not fear him, but the one who extends that power to him. Nevertheless, this should not be an excuse to undermine Satan's power and authority on this earth. After all, the Bible calls him "the ruler of this world" (John 12:31; 14:30; 16:11); "the god of this world" (2 Corinthians 4:4); "the prince of the power of the air" (Ephesians 2:2); and a "cosmic power over this present darkness" (Ephesians 6:12). His thousands of supernatural evil subordinates and partners are called "demons" (Matthew 8:3; James 2:19), "evil spirits" (Luke 7:21), "unclean spirits" (Matthew 10:1), and "the devil and his angels" (Matthew 25:41).

We see God's absolute power and authority when Jesus simply said "Go" in Matthew 8:29-32 when the demons begged Jesus, "If you drive us out, send us into the herd of pigs" (NIV). One word is all it takes God to show who is really in charge. But we should still take Satan and his associates very seriously.

Principle no. 4. God can use Satan to accomplish His ultimate will by simply giving permission to Satan to do that which Satan already desires to do.

Job 1: 8 shows us how God is confident in Job; we also get a sense that God is trying to test Job's faith. One story that shows how God's authority extends even over Satan, and God uses Satan to accomplish His ultimate will is the story of David. We find two accounts of the same story of David ordering to count the fighting men of Israel. One account is in 2 Samuel 24:1, and the other account is in 1 Chronicles 21:1. In 2 Samuel 24:1, God incited David to number Israel because God was angry with David. Ultimately, God wanted to teach David not to trust in his number of fighting men, but to trust in Him. So, He moved to let David count the fighting men of Israel, and in 1 Chronicles 21:1, He used Satan to do it.

The crucifixion of Jesus Christ is another example. It was clearly the hand of Satan that played a role in the crucifixion of Jesus Christ, as it is written in Luke 22:1-3, "Now the Festival of Unleavened Bread, called the Passover, was approaching, and the chief priests and the teachers of the law were looking for some way to get rid of Jesus, for they were afraid of the people. Then Satan entered Judas, called Iscariot, one of the Twelve" (NIV). It was certainly not in Satan's authority to take Jesus's life. Jesus said in Luke 22:22, "The Son of Man will go as it has been decreed. But woe to that man who betrays him!" (NIV). In John 10:18 Jesus said, "No one takes it from me, but I lay it down of my own accord. I have authority to lay it down and authority to take it up again. This command I received from my Father" (NIV). No one killed Jesus, neither the Jews, nor the Romans, nor Satan. Jesus gave His life willfully only to take it back. It was His obedience to the Father that brought Him from heaven to earth; His love that took Him to the cross; and His power that rose Him up on the third day.

Principle no. 5. God is sovereign over Satan's lies, temptations, and deceptions. Jesus said, "You belong to your father, the devil, and you want to carry out your father's desires. He was a murderer from the beginning, not holding to the truth, for there is no truth in him. When he lies, he speaks his native language, for he is a liar and the father of lies" (John 8:44 NIV).

It is Satan's nature to lie to us and convince us that all suffering is bad and that God is causing all of the pain and suffering to make us feel that we are worthless. He does this in order to persuade us to forsake worshiping God. He desires that we worship him rather than God, but he is content with us simply not worshipping God.

Satan's utmost desire is that we somehow turn away from God. Whether it is by distracting us with health and wealth or a lack of both, or inflicting pain in our lives or in the lives of our loved ones. He never stops finding ways to shift our focus from God to something or someone else. Sometimes he influences loved ones to inspire us and motivate us to go against God. We read in Job 2:8-10, "And he took him a potsherd to scrape himself with; and he sat down among the ashes. Then said his wife to him, Do you still retain your integrity? curse God, and die. But he said to her, You speak as one of the foolish women speaks. What? shall we receive good at the hand of God, and shall we not receive evil? In all this did not Job sin with his lips" (NASB).

When we do not rely on God's sovereignty, the tempter can take us over; just in the way that he entered into Judas Iscariot, he enters into us as well (Luke 22:3-4). The true understanding of God's sovereignty which Job understood can only be obtained if we fix our eyes on the author of life, our Lord Jesus Christ, regardless of the circumstances in which we may find ourselves. In Job 1:21-22, we witness the essence of Job's faith when he denounces his association with materialistic possessions, including his very own children. In one statement, he made it clear that, whether he lives or dies, whether he has worldly things or not, he will continue to praise the name of God. He said, "Naked I came from my mother's womb, and naked I will depart. The LORD gave and the LORD has taken away; may the name of the LORD be praised" (Job 1:21 NIV). The Bible says, "In all of this, Job did not sin by charging God with wrongdoing" (Job 1:22 NIV).

Over and over again, the Bible testifies that Job did not sin against God in his time of trouble. This is why James uses the example of Job to teach the church how to persevere in the face of trials and tribulations. He writes, "Behold, we consider those blessed who remained steadfast. You have heard of the steadfastness of Job, and you have seen the purpose of the Lord, how the Lord is compassionate and merciful" (James 5:11ESV). We should imitate Job when confronted with the problem of suffering and pain.

Endnotes

52 Tim Burt, "Fresh Manna," An Inspiring Story-Horatio G. Spafford, http://todays-freshmanna.wordpress.com/2010/11/09/an-inspiring-story-horatio-g-spafford/ (accessed July 1, 2014).

53 John Piper, Ten Aspects of God's Sovereignty Over Suffering and Satan's Hand in It, Desiring God 2005 National Conference

Chapter 28
God and Our Suffering

Regardless of knowing who is responsible for the evil in this world and regardless of our suffering and pain, we often ignore the plank in our own eye; we are responsible for much of the destruction in this world, and we have ushered in many of the problems we face individually and collectively because of our poor decisions. As the Bible says, because of our "evil desires," we tend to look for a speck in God's eye, to criticize Him, and to accuse Him for many of the bad things that have happened to us. In doing so, we wrong ourselves, others, this world, and, above all, we wrong God. Here are seven lessons we learn from Job's life.

Lesson no. 1. God is not afraid of our questions, but it hurts Him when we doubt His plans and promises for us.

In Job 40:2 we read, "Will the one who contends with the Almighty correct him? Let him who accuses God answer him!" (LIV). God's response to us as believers is this: If you say, "Why God, why me?" like Job, we become victims of our own understanding of God, trying to put the God of the universe into a little box. We tend to define God and redefine Him as needed. We associate attributes that should not be associated with Him. When confronted with pain and suffering, we think that He must hate us, that He must be our enemy, and that He is punishing us even though we are His children.

Theology is a good thing, but it can be the venom of the ancient serpent without the truth of God. Job indeed was a wise and faithful man; he understood many of the things around him, but when it came to the everlasting love of God, he too became the prey of the old tricks of Satan. In Job chapter 13, Job tells his friends, who have been accusing him of all kinds of things, "You, however, smear me with lies; you are worthless physicians, all of you! If only you would be altogether silent! For you, that would be wisdom" (NIV). Yet he could not keep silent to hear from God or to understand why God was doing what He was doing. He bought into the lies of Satan gradually for a short time. We do the same when troubles come. In the beginning, we seem strong, we depend on God, but, as it gets harder, we defile His name or at least stop trusting in the way that we should.

Lesson no. 2. God is not our enemy, and we should not always listen to others because not everyone who speaks about God is a child of God.

Job 13:1-3 tells us what it was that Job was misunderstanding about the sovereignty of God. He tells his friends, "My eyes have seen all this, my ears have heard and understood it. What you know, I also know; I am not inferior to you. But I desire to speak to the Almighty and to argue my case with God" (NIV). He was convinced that it was God who was against him and punishing him. At first, he was not able to believe, but, the more he heard the lies of Satan, the more he believed in them. He forgot that God is sovereign over all of the lies and deceptions of Satan; he forgot that God's sovereignty prevails over all of the plans, tricks, and trials of Satan only if one remains faithful to God and listens to Him. God speaks even in the midst of the most painful atrocities.

Lesson no. 3. God is God, and He knows best what He is doing and why. We cannot fight our way out by arguing with God.

Job was sure that he would be vindicated if he reasoned and argued with God. In Job 13:15-18, when talking to his friends about God, Job said, "Though he slay me, yet will I hope in him; I will surely defend my ways to his face. Indeed, this will turn out for my deliverance, for no godless person would dare come before him! Listen carefully to what I say; let my words ring in your ears. Now that I have prepared my case, I know I will be vindicated"(NIV). Moving forward, Job turns it up a notch. He forgets in his pride as who he is addressing and starts playing the flute of his own righteousness—a reaction we can all relate to, especially when trials test our faith. Job goes on to say in Job 13:19, "Can anyone bring charges against me? If so, I will be silent and die" (NIV). Then he presents a human solution to God; he calls for a truce by suggesting in Job 13:20-22, "Only grant me these two things, God, and then I will not hide from you: Withdraw your hand far from me, and stop frightening me with your terrors. Then summon me and I will answer, or let me speak, and you reply to me" (NIV). And finally the biggest blunder of all—he calls upon God for evidences of his unrighteousness, "How many wrongs and sins have I committed? Show me my offense and my sin" (NIV).

It is easy to get into an argument with our righteous God and demand evidence for why He is punishing us. Even though God was not the source of our suffering, by challenging His justice and proclaiming our righteousness, we offend God and commit the sin of pride and self-righteousness.

Lesson no. 4. God's sovereignty rules out any possibility of second guesses.

Jeremiah 29:11 says, "For I know the plans I have for you, declares the LORD, plans for welfare and not for evil, to give you a future and a hope" (ESV). It is ironic that this promise falls in the middle of God's 70-year judgment. Verdict: "You did not listen to me?" Later in his account, Jeremiah puts a yoke on his neck to symbolize God's judgment of bondage to Nebuchadnezzar, the king of Babylon. In Job 40:8 God said, "Would you discredit my justice? Would you condemn me to justify yourself" (NIV). God in His sovereignty knew exactly what was going on in Job's heart and mind because it is written "Would not God have discovered it, since He knows the secrets of the heart?" (Psalm 44:21 NIV). Jesus in His earthly ministry said, "You are the ones who justify yourselves in the eyes of others, but God knows your hearts. What people value highly is detestable in God's sight" (Luke 16:15 NIV). In Jeremiah 17:10, God said, "I the Lord search the heart and examine the mind, to reward each person according to their conduct, according to what their deeds deserve" (NIV). This is exactly why, in Matthew 22:37-39, when asked what the greatest commandment was, Jesus said, "Love the Lord your God with all your heart and with all your soul and with all your mind. This is the first and greatest commandment" (NIV) of course quoting from Deuteronomy 6:5. Then he joined another command from Leviticus 19:18, and completed His answer, "and the second is like it: 'love your neighbor as yourself.' All the law and the Prophets hang on these two commandments" (Matthew 22:39-40 NIV).

Jesus was concerned with our understanding of God's sovereignty-that in God's economy, everything is already unfolding according to God's will and plan. You and I may never see the full picture, but that should not be a reason to divide God's actions into good and bad. There is no need for God to think twice, to think about a backup plan, or to second guess Himself to fix a problem. Although some would treat Moses's Ten Commandments separately, the first being our duty to God and the second being our duty to other men. Jesus's answer put the first three together because they instruct us how to love God. The next seven commandments then show us how to love our neighbors. One of the ways to look at Matthew 22:37-39 is that there is more emphasis on how we treat other men than on how we treat God because men can tell you to your face how you are treating them and how you are behaving. Here you have an equal level of intelligence where you can argue and reason, whereas, in God's case you may justify your actions as you wish, but that would be foolish because you can never understand Him fully.

Like Job we all try to discredit God's justices and condemn Him for letting bad things happen to us; we protest, asking why bad things happen to good people. We are very helpful when someone else is going through pain and suffering, but when it is our turn, we often do not measure up to the standard we would hope for from other Christians.

Lesson no. 5. Through suffering and pain, God bring us to complete submission and surrender.

Our complete surrender and submission is only possible when we allow God to complete His plan. Philippians 1:6 says, "Being confident of this, that he who began a good work in you will carry it on to completion until the day of Christ Jesus" (NIV). Regardless of what Job, his friends, or even we thought about the suffering of Job, in God's perfect plan it was a just act in two ways: 1) It was just to Satan because he did not have the opportunity to test Job's faith amidst God's hedge around him (Job 1:10). 2) It would not have been just to Job if he wouldn't have been given the chance to learn what he did about the sovereignty of God by the end of his trials. We see in Job 42:6, he confesses, "My ears had heard of you but now my eyes have seen you. Therefore I despise myself and repent in dust and ashes" (NIV).

Lesson no. 6. God always has a purpose behind our suffering, whether we see it or not.

Job's suffering and pain began with a simple reason: God wanted to show Satan (and other heavenly beings) that His man, Job, would worship Him regardless of whether or, not he had all of his possessions, family, and good health. These three things are so precious to human beings—our health, our wealth, and our family. But God saw something else that was hidden from everyone's eyes, including Job's own—the seed of pride. It is very pride that ignited rebellion in heaven in the ancient days, when Lucifer and his followers were pushed and thrown out of heaven. This pride was sitting deep in Job's heart.

According to Elihu, Job's younger friend, God allowed suffering to purge Job's heart of the residue of pride that had lain quietly. As the story unfolds, and the days of Job's misery prolonged and intensified, his pain increased, and we see a clear weakness in his confidence that God was for him. In order to answer the allegations and wrong reasons that were presented by Eliphaz, Bildad, and Zophar, Job said things about God that were not true. He began to insist on his own righteousness at the expense of God's justice.

Here in lies another purpose: to rebuke Job from his bad theology and wrong understanding of God's mercy and love. As Isaiah 64:6 says, "All of us have become like one who is unclean, and all our righteous acts are like filthy rags we all shrivel up like a leaf, and like the wind our sins sweep us away" (NIV).

Lesson no. 7. God does not want us to go through suffering and say nothing because might is right.

In Job 40:9 says, "Do you have an arm like God's, and can your voice thunder like his?" (NIV). Like Job, it is presumptuous of us to assume that things can be done differently than God has dictated, as if we have seen the millions and billions of things that God does in a day to run this world. God's questions to Job paint a clear picture, showing us that we have no idea what it takes to make decisions about how to run the world for God's glory and for the joy of God's people. God's might is not arbitrary but purposeful; it is always to uphold His glory by simultaneously blessing the meek and humble and bringing down the prideful and arrogant.

Yet God invites us to discover Him, and seek Him. God asked Job primarily three types of questions: questions about the world below; (Job 38:4-18) questions about the world above (Job 38: 21-38); and questions about the world animals (Job 38:39-30).

John Piper writes,

> *So whether we focus on the earth or the sea or the dawn or the snow or hail or constellations or rain. The upshot is that Job is ignorant and impotent. He doesn't know where they came from. He doesn't know how to make them work. He is utterly surrounded, above and below, by mysteries. And so are we, because the scientific advancements of the last two hundred years are like sand-pails of saltwater hauled from the ocean of God's wisdom and dumped in a hole on the beach while the tide is rising.*[54]

I have drawn a few conclusions regarding Why God Allows Suffering and why sometimes it comes from the hands of God:

Conclusion no. 1. To show his glory before others, Jesus was asked by his disciples about a man who was blind from his birth, "Rabbi, who sinned, this man or his parents, that he was born blind?" Jesus answered, "It was not that this man sinned, or his parents, but that the works of God might be displayed in him" (John 9:1-3 ESV).

Conclusion no. 2. To teach us and instruct us in something that we would never know of or understand otherwise.

Conclusion no. 3. To draw us near to him.

Conclusion no. 4. To strengthen our faith.

Therefore, no matter how hard it gets, never let this world lie to you saying that God does not care. He does care, otherwise why would He send His only Son to die on the cross for us and to reconcile us back to Himself?

When life gets harder, remember that you worship a God who is sovereign over all circumstances; He is sovereign over life and death, and He is also sovereign over Satan and all of his tricks and trials.

When you do not find hope and find yourself questioning God, believing in false teachings about Him, or condemning Him or yourself, remember that you have an advocate in Heaven who intercedes on your behalf. He promises that all of your pain and suffering will pass away, and you will enjoy an everlasting life with Him.

Endnotes

54 John Piper, Ten Aspects of God's Sovereignty Over Suffering and Satan's Hand in It, Desiring God 2005 National Conference

Part Seven

Christianity Among Other Religions

Chapter 29
Righteous Suffering in Christ

One of the fundamental differences that can be verified through historical data is the suffering of Christians for Christ. This sets Christian apart from every other religion. As Christ suffered for the Church, similarity the Church suffers for Christ's namesake. Christian suffering is referred to as persecution. The following two chapters look at the writings of the Church Fathers, scholars, theologians, and historians as well as at Scripture to present a concise overview of Christian persecution. By reviewing this information in these two chapters, I present the factual reality of persecution throughout history as well as in recent times. I will discuss some of the most critical issues pertaining to Christian persecution that have provoked people from all backgrounds to investigate and analyze the phenomenon of the voluntary act of dying by the masses around the world for simply believing in Christ. Stories of those who willfully gave their lives for the cause of their Christian faith without pursuing financial, political, or government agendas provide a unique perspective that has served as a guiding and assessing tool.

It has been over 2,000 years since the founder of the Christian faith, Jesus of Nazareth, was arrested, tried, sentenced to death, crucified, buried, and, as Christians believe, raised again on the third day as He foretold in Luke 18:31-34. His resurrection became the pivotal point in Christianity that determined the fate of those who would follow Him—as He said, "and you will be hated by all for my name's sake. But the one who endures to the end will be saved" (Matthew 10:22 ESV). On the subject of suffering and martyrdom, Josef Tson writes:

> He [Jesus] expects them to meet that hatred with love, and to face that violence with glad acceptance, following His example by suffering and dying for the lost world. Their suffering and martyrdom are prompted by their allegiance to His own Person and are endured for the purpose of spreading His gospel. Christ's disciples do not seek these things for their own sake, and they do not inflict these on themselves. Their goal is not to suffer and to die; on the contrary, their goal is Christ's Person and Christ's cause in the world, the spreading of His gospel.[55]

In the aftermath of the crucifixion and resurrection of Christ, the persecution of His followers continues and becomes steadily worse. Subsequently, Christian persecution in modern times is much worse than ever before, yet many people in the West are totally unaware that Christians in the East are being killed, raped, and deprived of basic human rights just because they are Christians. "Why has the suffering of the Middle Eastern Christian communities not ignited outrage and support from Western Christians? The answer has something to do with Israel and the Second Coming," writes Professor Diarmaid MacCulloch.[56]

Historical Evidence of Persecution: Historical evidence of Christian persecution is available both in Christian and non-Christian writings. The first Christian martyr, Stephen, who died for Christ's sake, received his ordination as a deacon in Acts 6:5 and was stoned to death in Acts chapter 7. Acts 12:2

describes the death of James, the brother of John by saying that he was "put to death with the sword" (Acts 12:2, NIV), and Peter was also arrested by Herod, but he was miraculously delivered only to be arrested again and killed by the Roman government. All of the apostles except for John were martyred for their faith.[57] The martyrdom did not stop there but continued throughout the centuries up until modern times.

The early Church father, Ignatius, the third bishop of Antioch in Syria, wrote a series of letters to several different churches on his way to martyrdom in Rome during the times of Emperor Trajan, between AD 98 and AD 117.[58] He wrote to Polycarp, the Bishop of the Church of the Smyrnaeans, in present-day Turkey, who would be executed soon after Ignatius. He wrote, "It is fitting, O Polycarp, most blessed in God, to assemble a very solemn council, and to elect one whom you greatly love, and know to be a man of activity, who may be designated the messenger of God; and to bestow on him this honour that he may go into Syria, and glorify your ever active love to the praise of Christ."[59]

It is notable that Ignatius's letter was about encouraging the church and talking about the Christian life that a follower of Jesus should live. He does not talk about his impending execution. It was considered to be an honor to die for Christ, as it was foretold by Christ that His true disciples would be insulted, persecuted and killed for His name's sake (Matthew 5:10; Luke 6:22; John 15:21). After the martyrdom of Ignatius, Polycarp wrote to the Philippians:

> *Now I beseech you all to obey the word of righteous-*
> *ness, and to endure with all the endurance which you*
> *also saw before your eyes, not only in the blessed*
> *Ignatius, and Zosimus, and Rufus, but also in others*

among yourselves, and in Paul himself, and in the other Apostles; being persuaded that all of these "ran not in vain," but in faith and righteousness, and that they are with the Lord in the "place which is their due," with whom they also suffered. For they did not "love this present world" but him who died on our behalf, and was raised by God for our sakes.[60]

The question that is often raised is, "Why are Christian persecuted?" From the writings of Church fathers, historians, and scholars, the answer is very simply that they were hated because of their anti-social behavior, meaning that they had a higher level of moral and ethical standards than was demanded by their present day. "They're different. They are a people that, in a way, declare their boundaries over against the larger society by their very rituals that lead to conversion—turning away from the gods and turning to the one God."[61]

Pliny the Younger, the governor of Pontus and Bithynia from 111-113, wrote to Emperor Trajan about Christians whom he persecuted:

They [Christians] asserted, however, that the sum and substance of their fault or error had been that they were accustomed to meet on fixed day before dawn and sign responsively a hymn to Christ as to a god, and to bind themselves by oath, not to some crime, but not to commit fraud, theft, or adultery, not falsify their trust, nor to refuse to return a trust when called upon to do so. When this was over, it was their custom to depart and to assemble again to partake of food—but ordinary and innocent food. Even this, they affirmed, they had ceased to do after my edict by which, in accordance with your instructions, I had forbidden political associations. Accordingly, I judged it all the more necessary to find out what the truth was by torturing two female slaves who were called deaconesses. But I discovered nothing else but depraved, excessive superstition.[62]

Since it was promised and foretold by Jesus Christ that persecution would continue until His return, it would be unrealistic to hope for the persecuted Church to think that the persecution would end soon. However, this should not prevent the un-persecuted church from being a voice for the voiceless. In the East, persecution is common. It is a part of one's life; no one expects it to end. People have the choice to abandon their faith and live freely, yet Christians choose to live in this oppression and to stand firm in the hope of Jesus Christ. In the West, however, particularly in the United States, there are two major problems regarding the phenomenon of martyrdom in the face of persecution. First, Americans have a hard time understanding how people could possibly be willing to take the life of another based only on their religious differences. Second, even though the church in the West has not experienced persecution in modern times, they often talk about persecution as if they know for sure that it is a good and blessed thing for the persecuted church.

The Church in the United States keeps her distance and provides theological reasoning and justification for the pain and suffering that the persecuted Church experiences, rather than standing up for them and demanding justice. "More Christians have died for their faith in this current century than all other centuries of church history combined." This might be due to the increase in the world population, but nevertheless Christians remain the most persecuted of all religious groups today.[64] Barbara Boland discusses the data from the Pew Research Center, writing, "Across the six years that Pew has conducted the study, Christians were being harassed for their faith in 151 countries and Muslims in 135. Together they represent the world's two largest religious groups and more than half of the world's population."[65]

Kirsten Powers, in her article "A Global Slaughter of Christians, but America's Churches Stay Silent" writes:

> *Christians are being singled out and massacred from Pakistan to Syria to the Nairobi shopping mall. ...Christians in the Middle East and Africa are being slaughtered, tortured, raped, kidnapped, beheaded, and forced to flee the birthplace of Christianity. One would think this horror might be consuming the pulpits and pews of American churches. Not so. The silence has been nearly deafening.*[66]

Endnotes

55 Josef Tson, Suffering and Martyrdom: God's Strategy in the World (Pasadena: William Carey Library, 2009), 195.

56 The Daily Beast, Why Won't the West Defend Middle Eastern Christians? http://www.thedailybeast.com/articles/2013/10/27/why-won-t-the-west-defend-middle-eastern-christians.html (accessed July 9, 2014).

57 Ken Curtis, "Whatever Happened to the Twelve Apostles," Christianity.com, http://www.christianity.com/church/church-history/timeline/1-300/whatever-happened-to-the-twelve-apostles-11629558.html, (accessed June 25, 2014).

58 Kirsopp Lake, "The Apostolic Fathers," Introduction to Ignatius of Antioch. Early Christian Writings, 1912, http://www.earlychristianwritings.com/ignatius-intro.html, (accessed June 25, 2014).

59 Ibid.

60 Polycarp, "The Apostolic Fathers," Polycarp. Early Christian Writings, http://www.earlychristianwritings.com/text/polycarp-lake.html, (accessed June 25, 2014).

61 Wayne A. Meeks, "The Martyrs" Frontline from Jesus to Christ, PBS, http://www.pbs.org/wgbh/pages/frontline/shows/religion/why/martyrs.html, (accessed June 25, 2014).

62 Pliny the Younger, "Letters 10/96-97" Pliney the Younger and Trajan on the Christians, Early Christian Writings, http://www.earlychristianwritings.com/text/pliny.html, (accessed June 25, 2014).

63 Dan Wooding, "Modern Persecution," Christianity.com, http://www.christianity.com/church/church-history/timeline/1901-2000/modern-persecution-11630665.html , (accessed June 25, 2014).

64 "Religious Hostilities Reach Six-Year High, PewResearch Religion & Public Life Project. http://www.pewforum.org/2014/01/14/religious-hostilities-reach-six-year-high/ (accessed June 25, 2014).

65 Barbara Boland, "Pew Study: Christians Are The World's Most Oppressed" Cnsnews.com, February 6, 2014, http://cnsnews.com/news/article/barbara-boland/pew-study-christians-are-world-s-most-oppressed-religious-group, (accessed June 25, 2014).

66 Kirsten Powers, "A Global Slaughter of Christians, but America's Churches Stay Silent" The Daily Beast. September 27, 2013, http://www.thedailybeast.com/articles/2013/09/27/a-global-slaughter-of-christians-but-america-s-churches-stay-silent.html (accessed June 25, 2014).

Chapter 30
The Purpose of Christian Suffering/Persecution

Many Western speakers, writers, and preachers are pushing the theme that Christianity grows in the midst of persecution. They base their analyses solely on the fact that Christianity grew in the early centuries because of persecution. In doing so, they are utterly disconnecting from the present day reality that the Church is becoming extinct in many of the parts of the world, particularly in the Middle East and the Islamic world, because of persecution. Christians in the West err in their understanding of—and, therefore, lack tangible support for—the persecuted church. Darmaid McCulloch writes:

> Christian communities were already generally in steep decline in numbers through the region, and Israel/ Palestine in particular, even before the present Syrian and Egyptian crises. Caught between the animosities of a politics which has other concerns, Arab Christians have every incentive to leave, whenever they can, for exile in less dangerous lands, ending a connection with homelands which goes directly back to the first generations of the followers of Christ. It is easy for them to feel abandoned and betrayed by the Christian-based cultures of the West. When will this Western silence end?[67]

It was true in the past that Christianity grew in the midst of persecution when indigenous churches were comfortable with their spiritual life, and the mission field was wide open to receiving missionaries. In the first century, it was needed because there were very few Christians, and they needed to be scattered in order to bring the Christian faith (Gospel message) to other parts of the world. Once considered an offshoot of the Jewish faith, Christianity became a completely independent faith in the aftermath of the destruction of the Jewish Temple in AD 70. Mark A. Noll describes the destruction of the temple and the persecution of Christians as the "great turning point" that "moved Christianity outward, to transform it from a religion shaped in nearly every particular by its early Jewish environment into a religion advancing toward universal significance in the broader reaches of the Mediterranean world, and then beyond."[68] He also states, "The blows that Vespasian, Titus, Hadrian, and other Roman generals rained upon Jerusalem did not destroy the Church. Rather, they liberated the church from its destiny as a universal religion offered to the whole world."[69]

Today, however, as the Church in many countries continues to be eradicated by the majority belief system (especially in the Islamic world), it would be an aggressive statement to say it is happening so that the church may grow. Grow to what extent? Should it grow in numbers or in faith? Besides, the epicenter of such ongoing persecution is in the East, whereas the church in the West enjoys freedom, prosperity and has never experienced persecution for her faith. It would be easy for Western Christians to say that persecution is good for the church, and that it allows the Church to grow. This is merely an excuse to not do anything for those who are being persecuted.

Richard Wurmbrand points out that, "Persecution has always produced a better Christian—a soul-winning Christian."[70] This is the most accurate understanding of the purpose of persecution. He writes, "Underground Christians rejoice on those rare occasions when they meet a serious Christian from the West!"[71] This is because the serious Christians would understand the true purpose of persecution and their place in that persecution.

The only true justification for such ongoing persecution from its inception is that it brings believers into a close fellowship with God and each other, as He is all they have to rely upon. Promise of Persecution: Tony Lane notices two major turning points in the life of the early Church. The first came in AD 70 when Christians were forced to abandon their identities as Nazarenes and "could be seen as a Jewish sect, alongside the Pharisees, the Sadducees, and the Essenes" (Acts 24:4),[72] and the second came when Emperor Constantine converted to Christianity in 312. "Until this time, the church was a dissenting minority, intermittently persecuted."[73] Constantine effectively ended the persecution. Richard Wurmbrand suggests, "By converting those who persecute Christians, we would free not only their victims, but the persecutors themselves."[74]

Persecution may have stopped by the government in the Roman Empire, but it continued outside of it by other governments as well as within the Empire by the Catholic Church. This is because church persecution was foretold by the head of the church, Jesus Christ Himself; therefore, it can never stop until He returns. In Matthew 5:11, Jesus said, "Blessed are you when people insult you, persecute you and falsely say all kinds of evil against you because of me" (NIV). In Matthew 10:17 Jesus said "Be on your guard; you will be handed over to the local councils and be flogged in the synagogues" (NIV). In Matthew 10:22 we find him furthering His promise. "You will be hated by everyone because of me, but the one who stands firm to the end will be saved" (NIV). In John 15:18, Jesus explained why those who follow Him would be hated, arrested, tortured and killed. He said, "If the world hates you, keep in mind that it hated me first" (NIV). He continued, and in verse 19 of John 15 says, "If you belonged to the world, it would love you as its own. As it is, you do not belong to the world, but I have chosen you out of the world. That is why the world hates you" (NIV), and in verse 21 of John 15, "They will treat you this way because of my name, for they do not know the one who sent me" (NIV).

Despite all of this, Jesus also promised that if Christians endure until the end, they will be saved and will be given crowns in heaven (Matthew 24:13; Matthew 10:22; Luke 21:19; Revelation 2:10). Therefore, the early church lived in anticipation of the second coming of Christ, and they feared no one and wanted for nothing. The following portion of a letter from an eye-witnesses of the martyrdom of Polycarp describes how Christians willfully and happily embraced death for the sake of Christ in the hope of the resurrected life in Christ:

> *Blessed, therefore, and noble are all the testimonies that happened according to the will of God, for it is right that we should be the more careful, and should ascribe unto God the authority over all things. For who would not admire their nobility and endurance and obedience? who, though they were torn with stripes so that the internal arrangement of their flesh became evident even as far as the veins and arteries within, endured it, so that even the bystanders compassionated them and bemoaned them; and that others even arrived at such a pitch of nobility that none of them would either sob or groan, showing all of us that in that hour the martyrs of Christ departed being tortured in the flesh, or rather that the Lord, standing by, associated himself with them. And applying them-*

*selves to the grace of Christ, they despised the torture
of this world, purchasing by the endurance of a single
hour remission from eternal punishment; and the fire
of their harsh tormentors was cold to them, for they
had before their eyes to escape the eternal and never-
quenched fire; and with the eyes of their heart they
looked up to the good things that are reserved for
those that endure, which neither hath ear heard, nor
eye seen, nor hath it entered into the heart of man; but
which were shown by the Lord unto them, who were
no longer men, but already angels.*[75]

When persuaded and pressed by the proconsul to deny Christ,
Polycarp said, "Eighty and six years have I served him, and in
nothing hath he wronged me; and how, then, can I blaspheme my
King, who saved me?" Consequently, he was burned alive. In
modern times, when Richard Wurmbrand was imprisoned for his
faith, when he abandoned atheism to follow Christ, he was asked
by political officers harshly, "How long will you continue to keep
your stupid religion?"[77] And he responded to them, "I have seen
innumerable atheists regretting on their deathbeds that they have
been godless; they called on Christ. Can you imagine that a Christian could regret, when death is near, that he has been a Christian
and call on Marx or Lenin to rescue him from his faith?"[78]

In the Annals of Tacitus, Tacitus reveals how Nero, in an
effort to hide his crime in which he planned a fire that destroyed
most of Rome, used Christians as a scapegoat.[79] He writes:

*Consequently, to get rid of the report, Nero fastened
the guilt and inflicted the most exquisite tortures on a
class hated for their abominations, called Christians
by the populace. Christus, from whom the name had its
origin, suffered the extreme penalty during the reign
of Tiberius at the hands of one of our procurators,*

> *Pontius Pilatus, and a most mischievous superstition, thus checked for the moment, again broke out not only in Judaea, the first source of the evil, but even in Rome, where all things hideous and shameful from every part of the world find their centre and become popular.*[80]

He paints the picture of persecution in the same manner as Scripture and as other Christian and non-Christian resources do. He writes:

> *Mockery of every sort was added to their deaths. Covered with the skins of beasts, they were torn by dogs and perished, or were nailed to crosses, or were doomed to the flames and burnt, to serve as a nightly illumination, when daylight had expired.*[81]

Endnotes

67 The Daily Beast, Why Won't the West Defend Middle Eastern Christians? http://www.thedailybeast.com/articles/2013/10/27/why-won-t-the-west-defend-middle-eastern-christians.html (accessed July 9, 2014).

68 Mark A Noll, Turning Points: Decisive Moments in the History of Christianity, Rev. ed. (Grand Rapids: Baker Academic, 2012), 17.

69 Ibid.,16.

70 Richard Wurmbrand, Tortured for Christ, 2nd ed. (Bartlesville: Living Sacrifice Book Company, 1998), 116.

71 Ibid.,114.

72 Tony Lane, A Concise History of Christian Thought, Rev. ed. (Grand Rapids: Baker Academic, 2006),4.

73 Ibid.,5.

74 Wurmbrand, Tortured for Christ, 113.

75 Charles H. Hoole, "The Martyrdom of Saint Polycarp, Bishop of Smyrna" The Martyrdom of Polycarp. Early Christian Writings, http://www.earlychristianwritings.com/text/martyrdompolycarp-hoole.html (accessed June 25, 2014).

76 Ibid.

77 Wurmbrand, Tortured for Christ, 102.

78 Ibid.

79 The accuracy of Tacitus's claim has been challenged on the basis of recent histor-ical research, at least as far as blaming Nero for the fire goes, however it is still undisputable that Nero did persecuted the church.

80 Tacitus, "The Annals of Tacitus" Early Christian Writings, http://www.early-christianwritings.com/text/annals.html (accessed June 25, 2014).

81 Ibid.

Chapter 31
What Differentiates Christianity from the Rest of the World's Religions?

There are many answers to this fundamental question when it comes to choosing a religion. However, the primary point of this book from the beginning has been that the more we know God and the more we understand Him, the better we realize that religions are not what God desires but true worshipers "...for they are the kind of worshippers the Father seeks. God is spirit, and his worshippers must worship in spirit and in truth" (John 4:23-24 NIV). If God was in the business of creating religion, He would have not created so many religions to confuse us all. God created man, and He commands man's soul and heart, "Love the Lord your God with all your heart and with all your soul and with all your strength and with all your mind; and 'Love your neighbor as yourself'" (Luke 10:27 NIV).

Christianity as a religion cannot accurately be compared to any other world religions because Jesus Christ did not intend to establish an institution when He came and died for us; therefore, the analysis of Christianity as an institution makes little sense. The mission and teaching of Christ differentiate Christianity from the rest of the world's religions, world-views, and belief systems. Christianity as a religion has failed over and over again and has driven people away because of the man made traditions, rituals, and partners, and it is likely that in the future it will continue to be a disappointment in this way. However, the mission and teachings of Jesus Christ will continue to liberate the captives and be the beacon of hope and eternal joy.

So if the question is not about Christianity as a religion but as a faith that represents the mission and teachings of Jesus Christ, then here are a few things that differentiate Christianity from other religions:

#1 Mission of Jesus Christ: It was a two-fold mission: the first part of His mission was to save us from ourselves, our sins, eternal punishment in Hell, and from God's wrath. The second part of His mission was to reconcile us back to our Heavenly Father (2 Corinthians 5:18-20). Jesus came to serve and not to be served (Matthew 20:28, Mark 10:45); He also came to be king (John 18:37); to bear witness to the truth (John 18:37); to fulfill the law (Matthew 5:17); to preach the Good News (Luke 4:43); for sinners (Mark 2:17, Luke 5:32, 1 Timothy 1:1,15); to put away sin (Hebrews 9:26, 1 John 3:5; John 1:29); to bear our sins (1 Peter 2:24, Hebrews 9:28); to heal the sick (Matthew 9:11-13, Mark 2:17); to give us life in abundance (John 10:7-10); to die for us, to give His life as a ransom (Matthew 20:28, Hebrews 9:26); to seek and save the lost (Luke 19:10); to reveal the Father (Matthew 11:27, John 14:9); to do the will of God (Hebrews 10:9); to bring fire and Judgment (Luke 12:49, Matthew 3:11-12, John 9:39, Luke 12:14, John 3:17, John 8:15); to be a faithful high priest (Hebrews 2:17); to destroy the work of the devil (1 John 3:8, Hebrews 2:14, John 12:31, John 14:30) and finally, He came to provide a pattern for life. Jesus said "learn from Me, for I am gentle and humble in heart" (Matthew 11:29), and if people do so faithfully, accepting His mission and the good news that He died that we may have life in Him for eternity, then we will be considered followers of Jesus Christ, Christians. "For to this you have been called, because Christ also suffered for you, leaving you an example, so that you might follow in his steps" (1 Peter 2:21 ESV).

#2 The purpose of Jesus Christ: It must be understood that the purpose of Jesus Christ was not to introduce a new set of rules and regulations to introduce a new branch of Judaism, to provide a new way to reach and please God, or even to make Himself the chief and commander of all previous religions. The purpose of Jesus's ministry, life, and sacrifice was above and beyond any known understanding of human reasoning. There are things that we simply may never fully comprehend. That is not because we are not intelligent enough, but merely because we are limited, mortal, and human. As it has been said before, Christianity is not a religion but a relationship with God through Christ Jesus, where man in his sinful nature cannot do anything to offend or to please God any longer. In this relationship, Jesus becomes the justification as well as the justifier, "He [God] did it to demonstrate His righteousness at the present time, so as to be just and the one who justifies those who have faith in Jesus" (Romans 3:26 NIV). Consequently, "all are justified freely by His grace through the redemption that came by Christ Jesus" (Romans 3:25).

It was no one else but God the Father Himself who presented Christ as a sacrifice of atonement for our sins, and it is written, "God presented Christ as a sacrifice of atonement, through the shedding of his blood—to be received by faith. He did this to demonstrate his righteousness, because in His forbearance He had left the sins committed beforehand unpunished" (Romans 3:36 NIV). In our finite knowledge, we cannot comprehend how God the father can demonstrate His righteousness by sacrificing

His son for our human atonement, but in God's infinite knowledge the atonement was the pivotal point in human history where God's love and wrath were pure at the same time through the cross and in Christ. "Yet it was the will of the LORD to crush him [Jesus]; he [God] has put him [Jesus] to grief; when his soul makes an offering for guilt" (Isaiah 53:10 ESV). We can raise questions such as, How could God the Father have killed His own Son, let alone be delighted to do so? What compelled the Father to do this? What compelled the Son to submit to this? According to Romans 2:23 "all have sinned and fall short of the glory of God" (NIV) and according to Romans 5:1 "Therefore having been justified by faith, we have peace with God through our Lord Jesus Christ" (NIV). Hence, the purpose of Jesus Christ' life and death was to please His father, to be obedient to Him even to death, to redeem the world, and to glorify God the Father.

In His words, Jesus prayed to His Father in John 17:1-5:

> *Father, the hour has come. Glorify your Son, that your Son may glorify you. For you granted him authority over all people that he might give eternal life to all those you have given him. Now this is eternal life: that they know you, the only true God, and Jesus Christ, whom you have sent. I have brought you glory on earth by finishing the work you gave me to do. And now, Father, glorify me in your presence with the glory I had with you before the world began (NIV).*

#3 Grace through Jesus Christ: At its core, Christianity is all about grace. Jesus Christ came into the world and redeemed mankind by reconciling them back to God, to glorify Him, and God the Father was well pleased. "And God placed all things under His [Jesus] feet and appointed him to be head over everything for the church" (Ephesians 1:22). In John 12:31-32, Jesus said, "Now the Son of Man is glorified and God is glorified in Him. If God is glorified in Him, God will glorify the Son in Himself, and will glorify Him at once" (ESV). This is why the Bible teaches about Jesus being "He is the radiance of the glory of God and the exact imprint of His nature" (Hebrews 1:3 ESV). There is nothing left that we as human beings can do or avoid doing that will enable us to escape the well deserved wrath of God because, in their mutual understanding, God and His Son provided a way to themselves through Christ. Paul writes,

> *He [Jesus] is before all things, and in Him all things hold together. He is also head of the body, the church; and He is the beginning, the firstborn from the dead, so that He Himself will come to have first place in everything. For it was the **Father's** good pleasure for all the fullness to dwell in Him, and through Him to reconcile all things to Himself, having made peace through the blood of His cross; through Him, **I say**, whether things on earth or things in heaven (Colossians 1:17-20 ESV).*

God's grace voids and nullifies all possibilities of man's effort to please or displease God to gain access to His throne. At the same time, the grace of God makes it possible for the religious and unreligious, the spiritual and unspiritual alike to access His throne equally, without any perception of self-righteousness based on human works. All He requires is the humility to forsake our pride and to understand that we have earned God's grace, or His pleasure. The Bible says, God did this "so that no one may boast before Him. It is because of Him that you are in Christ Jesus, who has become for us wisdom from God—that is, our righteousness, holiness and redemption" (1 Corinthians 1:29-30 NIV), "For it is by grace you have been saved, through faith—and this is not from yourselves, it is the gift of God—not by works, so that no one can boast" (Ephesians 2:8-9 NIV). "He saved us, not on the basis of deeds which we have done in righteousness, but according to His mercy, by the washing of regeneration and renewing by the Holy Spirit" (Titus 3:5 NASB).

What differentiates Christianity from other religions can be summed up in one verse, "You did not choose Me, but I choose you, and appointed you" (John 15:16 NASB).

Chapter 32
Which Branch of Christianity is Correct & What Church Should One Go To?

The day and age that we live in is not much different from the era when Jesus walked on this earth. He constantly rebukes the hypocrisy of religious leaders and exposes their filth and lack of care for the needy and poor. He rose to fame not because He was rich and popular among religious authorities but because of his radical teachings. He was a truthful, uncompromising, and authoritatively bold man. He was the embodiment of His own words. His teachings shook the very foundation of the social, religious, moral, and ethical fabric of His time. The ripple effect was so strong, dramatic, and drastic that still today, after 2,000 years, it continues to challenge our modern society in the twenty-first century.

It was not a crime that He committed that cost Jesus His life, but it was the radical teachings that He was preaching that threatened the religious and political leaders of His time. Christian was the name and title that was given to those who followed Christ and manifested the same radical change in their lifestyle. Here is the question that those who call ourselves Christians should ask ourselves, Do we really deserve the title?

If one says that he has received Christ and that he has a new relationship with God, I would then ask, "Do you have a new relationship with sin?" If you do not have a new relationship with sin, then you do not have a new relationship with God. Do you also have a new relationship with the Word of God? If you do not have a new relationship with the Word of God, then you do not have a new relationship with Christ.

If you look around, you will see that the truth of God is being distorted for personal gain by many. The Word of God has been twisted to accommodate a multitude of sin on its own terms in the Church. There is more emphasis on "Churchianity" than Christianity. The Church of Christ has been taken over by spiritualists, scientologists, traditionalists, and legalists. The truth of the Gospel is gasping in the coffin of rules and regulations; board meetings and agendas; criticism and entertainment; envy and malice; slander and gossip; jealousy and judgment. The religiosity of men and women who claim to be the followers of Christ are chasing His sheep away.

The house of God (a place where believers meet to worship God) is being robbed because the people of God have fallen asleep. The love of God seems to fade away not because He has forsaken His people but because we have left Him. We have become a lukewarm Church. Whether it is by committing the heinous crime against God of denying or altering His doctrine, or by not standing against the one who preaches the false gospel of health and wealth, happiness and prosperity have been lost at the cost of innocent souls.

We all have failed Him over and over again. We have violated His sanctity and trust. Western civilization, for the first time in its history, is in danger of dying. The reason is spiritual. It is losing its life and its soul, and that soul is the Christian faith. That radical faith that made us into a nation that welcomes all those who suffer because of their belief in Christ. The philosophical virus that is killing our society, civilization, and the very soul of Western existence is not multiculturalism or other faith, but the monoculturalism of secularism.

No faith, no soul, no God, no peace. Together, faithful and faithless secularists are defining and redefining words due to a lack of human desire to pursue and understand God's purpose and will in our lives and in this world.

Which church should one go to? Picking a church could be the second most important decision in your spiritual life. A church and its congregation provide a proper system of accountability for you, and this is the place where you will receive food for your soul, week after week. Many sincere seekers parish because of the teaching they receive in the churches they go to. If only they would have been a little more careful and diligent in inquiring after a Christ centered and Bible-believing church. There are many churches that might proclaim Christ and appeared to be Christian churches, but it is only the guidance of the Holy Spirit and your sensitivity to God's voice that can lead you to a place where you will be fed, edified, challenged, and, if needed, confronted, all in love to help you to grow even closer to God.

Evidence of Faith: One of the best ways to evaluate a church— whether she is from God and of God is by meeting and genuinely seeking the evidence of faith in the lives of the congregants and the leaders. You must understand that the evidence of faith is not what you produce, but it is the embodiment of your faith in the Lord Jesus Christ, a miraculous, supernatural work of God. In the Sermon on the Mount, the beatitudes are not what you do in order to be a Christian; rather, they are what Christians do as a result of supernatural changes in their lives. There are also clear benefits of such a miracle of faith in our lives, such as:

- **Benefit no. 1** — We receive eternal inheritance that comes through a relationship with God in Christ through His death.

- **Benefit no. 2** — We receive eternal inheritance as reward, not for what we have done or accomplished, but through Christ's labor on our behalf.

- **Benefit no. 3** — This all is done for us in the name of Jesus, thus...

- **Benefit no. 4** — We have been delivered from the power of darkness and have been rescued to be God's children in Christ. Therefore, Satan has no claim on Christians' lives.

- **Benefit no. 5** — We have been taken out of the road of death and Hell and put on the road of hope and the Lord, because He is Holy; therefore, Christians should live holy and just lives.

- **Benefit no. 6** — We have been redeemed and now belong to God.

- **Benefit no. 7** — We have been forgiven and now enjoy our renewed relationship with God.

Therefore, a church and a Christian should remember the following blessings:

1. We have been forgiven, and the way we can remember this is by reading God's Word and coming together to worship Him.

2. We have no obligation to sin because there is no sin that was not paid for in full by Jesus Christ.

3. We have no need to indulge ourselves in an useless conversation regarding how big a certain sin is because the grace of God through our Lord Jesus is sufficient for us and indeed bigger than any sin that we have ever committed.

4.   We have been justified so that we may be considered righteous before the holy God.

Regeneration: The Christian doctrine that is always lost and is always needed in dark times such as these is the doctrine of regeneration. Men are dead in their transgression. They cannot come to God because they will not come to God. The work of salvation must be preceded by a genuine, recreated, supernatural, dynamic work of the Holy Sprit in the heart of a person, a work that allows that person to see properly and might respond properly to the claims of the Gospel.

Paul Washer proposes:

> *Since repentance and faith are the result of a supernatural, a definite supernatural work of God, and since every work God begins He completes. And since the work of salvation is more than anything else about the declaration of God's power to the Universe that you can be assured that if God has saved a person He has changed that person in his very core of his being and he will continue working in that person to bring about sanctification and conformity to Christ. That is why it is absolutely absurd to believe that a man can be Christian and not be changed.*[82]

In short, a Christian, according to the Scriptures, is a new creature, and the evidence of a new creature is that you will witness and testify to the characteristics that Jesus mentioned in His Sermon on the Mount. A barren and unfruitful life that represents anything other than what the Gospel teaches is not and cannot be a Christian life.

Endnotes

82 Paul Washer, "The Cost of Discipleship" Faith Bible Church, September 18, 2009, http://media.sermonaudio.com/mediapdf/918091020561.pdf, (accessed July 2, 2014).

COMMITMENT/QUESTIONS
AND COMMENTS CARD

Last Name:

First Name:

Address:

Phone:

Email:

Check one or more:
- ❏ Acceptance of Christ   ❏ Assurance of Salvation
- ❏ Rededication   ❏ Inquiry

Do you attend a local church or campus fellowship?
❏ Yes   ❏ No

If yes, Church name:

If no, would you like to get connected with a church?
❏ Yes   ❏ No

Would you like to start a corresponding Bible course?
❏ Yes   ❏ No

Should we contact you?   ❏ Yes   ❏ No

My Comments: *(continue on back, if desired)*

_____I prayed to commit my life to Jesus Christ and enter faith today.

_____I commit to a journey to decide about Jesus and Christianity.

_____I am interested in a discussion group on the issue of

_____.

_____I am not ready to enter or journey toward Christian faith.

_____I am already a committed Christ-follower.

Cut out this card and mail it to:
AMBASSADORS MINISTRIES
123 West 57th Street
New York, NY 10019-2200

Would you like to contact us or get more information?
Email: ambassadors@cbcnyc.com
Phone: 212-975-0170 Ext. 109
www.alfonsejaved.com • www.cbcnyc.org

Reference & Resources List

Reference List

Anderson, Janna, and Lee Rainie, "Main Findings: Teens, technology, and human potential in 2020," February 29, 2012, *PewReseach Internet Project*. Accessed June 26, 2014.http://www.pewinternet. org/2012/02/29/main-findings-teens-technology-and-human-potential-in-2020/

Arnold, Matthew. *Culture and Anarchy.* New York: AMS Press, 1970.

American Hospital Association. *Hospital Statistics.* Chicago. 1999. See also: Brennan, Troyen A.; Leape, Lucian L.; Laird, Nan M., et al. Incidence of adverse events and negligence in hospitalized patients: Results of the Harvard Medical Practice Study I. N Engl J Med. 324:370–376, 1991. See also: Leape, Lucian L.; Brennan, Troyen A.; Laird, Nan M., et al. The Nature of Adverse Events in Hospitalized Patients: Results of the Harvard Medical Practice Study II. N Engl J Med. 324(6):377–384, 1991.

Blomber, Craig. *The Historical Reliability of the New Testament.* In Reasonable Faith, by William Lane Criag, 193-231. Westchester, Ill.: Crossway, 1994.

Borel, Emile. *Probability and Life, Dover Publications*, translated from the original, Les Probabilite et la Vie. New York:Dover Publications, 1962.

Boland, Barbara. "Pew Study: Christians Are The World's Most Oppressed." *Cnsnews.com*, February 6, 2014, Accessed June 25, 2014.http://cnsnews.com/news/article/barbara-boland/pew-study-christians-are-world-s-most-oppressed-religious-group,

Burt, Tim. *Fresh Manna*, An Inspiring Story-Horatio G. Spafford. Accessed July 1, 2014.http://todaysfreshmanna.wordpress.com/2010/11/09/an-inspiring-story-horatio-g-spafford/

C.S. Lewis, *The problem of Pain*. New York: HarperCollins Publishers, 1996.

Centers for Disease Control and Prevention (National Center for Health Statistics). *Births and Deaths: Preliminary Data for 1998*, National Vital Statistics Reports. 47(25): 1999: 6.

Hoole, Charles. H. "The Martyrdom of Saint Polycarp, Bishop of Smyrna" The Martyrdom of Polycarp. Early Christian Writings, Accessed June 25, 2014.http://www.earlychristianwritings.com/text/martyrdompolycarp-hoole.html.

Curtis, Ken. Whatever Happened to the Twelve Apostles. *Christianity. com*. Accessed June 25, 2014. http://www.christianity.com/church/church-history/timeline/1-300/whatever-happened-to-the-twelve-apostles-11629558.html.

Dietrich Bonhoeffer, *Barcelona Lectures*, December 11, 1928.

Dietrich Bonhoeffer, *A Testament to Freedom:The Essential Writings of Dietrich Bonhoeffer*. HarperCollins Publishers, 1990 & 1995.

Encyclopaedia Britannica, 8th ed., s.v. "Internet." Chicago: Encyclopaedia Britannica, 2014. Accessed June 25, 2014.http://www.britannica.com/EBchecked/topic/113978/choice.

Evans, Stephen. C. *Philosophy of Religion*. Downers Grove: InterVarsity Press, 1982.

Green, Clifford. J. and Michael DeJonge, *The Bonheoffer Reader*. Minneapolis: Fortress Press, 2013.

Guinness, Os. *Unspeakable: Facing up to the challenge of evil*. New York: HarperCollins Publishers, 2006.

Hoole, H. Charles. "The Martyrdom of Saint Polycarp, Bishop of Smyrna." The Martyrdom of Polycarp. Early Christian Writings, Accessed June 25, 2014.http://www.earlychristianwritings.com/text/martyrdompolycarp-hoole.html.

Houdmann, Michael. Did God create evil?, *Got Questions?org*. Accessed June 25, 2014. http://www.gotquestions.org/did-God-create-evil.html.

Institute of Medicine. *To Err Is Human: Building a Safer Health System*. Washington, DC: The National Academies Press, 2000.

Institute for Evidence-Based Cryonics, Scientists' *Open Letter on Cryonics*, Accessed June 25, 2014. http://www.evidencebasedcryonics.org/scientists-open-letter-on-cryonics/

Keller, Timothy. *The Reason for God: Belief in an Age of Skepticism*. New York: Dutton, 2008.

Lake, Kirsopp. "The Apostolic Fathers." Early Christian Writings, 1912,

Accessed June 25, 2014. http://www.earlychristianwritings.com/text/polycarp-lake.html.

Lane, Tony. *A Concise History of Christian Thought*, Rev. ed. Grand Rapids, MI: Baker Academic, 2006.

"Life's BIG questions" *The Problem of Suffering*, Accessed June 25, 2014. http://www.lifes-big-questions.org/Sect3Page2.php.

MacDonald, Gordon. *Rebuilding Your Broken World*. Nashvill: Thomas Nelson Publishers, 2003.

McCarthy Michael, *Man is fallen and will destroy the Earth – but at least we greens made him wait*, Friday 29 March 2013, Accessed June 25, 2014. http://www.independent.co.uk/voices/comment/man-is-fallen-and-will-destroy-the-earth-but-at-least-we-greens-made-him-wait-8554548.html.

Meeks, A.Wayne. "The Martyrs" Frontline from Jesus to Christ. *PBS*, Accessed June 25, 2014. http://www.pbs.org/wgbh/pages/frontline/shows/religion/why/martyrs.html.

Melton, James L. copyright 1995, tract: *The Second Coming of Jesus Christ*.

Metaxas, Eric. *Bonhoeffer: Pastor, Martyr, Prophet, Spy*. Thomas Nelson, 2010.

Moody, Raymond. *Life After Life: The Investigation of a Phenomenon--Survival of Bodily Death* New York: HarperCollins Publishers, 2001.

Micklethwaith, John and Adrian Wooldridge, *God is Back: How the global revival of faith is changing the world*. New York: The Penguin Press, 2009.

National Research Council. *The Arctic in the Anthropocene: Emerging Research Questions*. Washington, DC: The National Academies Press, 2014.

National Research Council. *Linkages Between Arctic Warming and Mid-Latitude Weather Patterns: Summary of a Workshop*. Washington, DC: The National Academies Press, 2014.

Nietzsche, Friedrich. "Is God Dead" Time. April 08, 1966. Accessed June 25, 2014. http://content.time.com/time/magazine/article/0,9171,835309,00.html.

Nietzsche, Friedrich. "Philosophy of suffering" Accessed June 25, 2014. http://www.angelfire.com/ut/inorbit/QuotesSuffering.html.

Nietzsche, Friedrich. *The Gay Science* (1882, 1887) para. 125; Walter

Kaufmann ed. New York: Vintage, 1974.

Noll, Mark A. *Turning Points: Decisive Moments in the History of Christianity*, 3rd ed. Grand Rapids, MI: Baker Academic, 2012.

Paul Washer, "The Cost of Discipleship" Faith Bible Church, September 18, 2009, Accessed July 2, 2014. http://media.sermonaudio.com/mediapdf/918091020561.pdf.

Piper, John. *Ten Aspects of God's Sovereignty Over Suffering and Satan's Hand in It*, Desiring God 2005 National Conference, October 7, 2005, Accessed June 25, 2014. http://www.desiringgod.org/conference-messages/ten-aspects-of-gods-sovereignty-over-suffering-and-satans-hand-in-it

Pliny the Younger, "Letters 10/96-97." Pliny the Younger and Trajan on the Christians. Early Christian Writings, Accessed June 25, 2014. http://www.earlychristianwritings.com/text/pliny.html.

Polycarp, "The Apostolic Fathers," Polycarp. Early Christian Writings, Accessed June 25, 2014. http://www.earlychristianwritings.com/text/polycarp-lake.html.

Powers, Kirsten. "A Global Slaughter of Christians, but America's Churches Stay Silent." The Daily Beast. September 27, 2013, Accessed June 25, 2014. http://www.thedailybeast.com/articles/2013/09/27/a-global-slaughter-of-christians-but-america-s-churches-stay-silent.html.

Princeton University, "Anselm's Ontological Argument" Accessed June 25, 2014. http://www.princeton.edu/~grosen/puc/phi203/ontological.html.

Quoted in A. N. Wilson, *God's Funeral*.New York: Norton, 1999.

Ramsey, Russel. B. "Shawshank Redmption (Frank Darabont, 1994)," Accessed June 25, 2014. http://www.ransomfellowship.org/article detail.asp?AID=221&B=Russell%20B.%20Ramsey&TID=2

"Religious Hostilities Reach Six-Year High." PewResearch Religion & Public Life Project. Accessed June 25, 2014. http://www.pewforum.org/2014/01/14/religious-hostilities-reach-six-year-high/

Schwarz, Bob. *You Came Unto Me: A Training Manual For Jail And Prison Ministry*. Harvest International Network.

"Scourging" Accessed June 25, 2014. http://the-crucifixion.org/scourging.htm#25

Stoner, Peter. W. *Science Speaks*. Chicago: Moody Bible Institute, 1968.

Tacitus, "The Annals of Tacitus." Early Christian Writings. Accessed June

25, 2014. http://www.earlychristianwritings.com/text/annals.html

"The Apostolic Fathers." Introduction to Ignatius of Antioch. Early Christian Writings, 1912, http://www.earlychristianwritings.com/ignatius-intro.html.

The Daily Beast, *Why Won't the West Defend Middle Eastern Christians?* Accessed June 25, 2014. http://www.thedailybeast.com/articles/2013/10/27/why-won-t-the-west-defend-middle-eastern-christians.html.

Tson, Josef. *Suffering and Martyrdom: God's Strategy in the World.* Pasadena: William Carey Library, 2009.

Turnbull, Nick. "Dewey's philosophy of questioning: science, practical reason and democracy," History of the Human Sciences 21. no.1 (2008): 49-75.

Wellman, Jack. "What are the Odds of Jesus' 700 Plus Prophecies Fulfillment?" *Yahoo Voice,* December 12, 2009. Accessed June 25, 2014. http://voices.yahoo.com/what-odds-jesus-700-plus-prophecies-fulfillment-5064980.html?cat=6

"What happens after death?" *Got Questions Ministries*, http://www.gotquestions.org/Biblical-inerrancy.html.

Wooding, Dan. "Modern Persecution." *Christianity.com.* http://www.christianity.com/church/church-history/timeline/1901-2000/modern-persecution-11630665.html.

Wonderslist, "10 Most Cruel Rulers Ever in History" Accessed June 25, 2014. http://www.wonderslist.com/10-most-cruel-rulers-ever-in-history/

Wurmbrand, Richard. *Tortured for Christ.* 2nd ed. Bartlesville: Living Sacrifice Book Company, 1998.

Resource List

1. Ahmad MG: Jesus in India., printed in Great Britain at the Alden Press, pp.20, Oxford 1978

2. Riceiotti G: The Life of Christ, Zizzamia Al (trans), Milwaukee, Bruce Publishing Co, 1947, pp.29-57, 78-153,161-167 & 586-647.

3. Bucklin R: The Legal and Medical Aspects of the Trial and Death of Christ, Sci Law 1970; 10: 14-26

4. McDowell J: The Resurrection Factor, San Bernardino, Calif, Here's Life Publishers, 1981, pp.20-53,75-103

5. Edwards WD, Gabel JG, Hosmer FE: On the Physical Death of Jesus Christ[as], JAMA 1986, 255: 1455-1463

6. Davis CT: The Crucifixion of Jesus: The Passion of Christ from a Medical Point of View, Ariz Med 1965; 22: 183-187

7. Barbet P: A Doctor at Calvary: The Passion of Our Lord Jesus Christ as Described by a surgeon, Earl of Wicklow (trans), Garden City, NY, Doubleday Image Books 1953, pp.12-18,37-147,159-175,187-208

8. Tenny SM: On death by crucifixion, Am Heart J 1964; pp.68: 286-287

9. Freidrich G: Theological Dictionary of the New Testament, Bremiley G (ed-trans) Grand Rapids, Mich, WB Eerdmans Publisher, 1971, Vol.7, pp.572, 573, 632

10. DePasquale NP, Burch GE: Death by crucifixion, Am Heart J 1963; pp.66: 434-435

11. Stroud W:Treatise on the Physical Cause of the Death of Christ and its Relation to the Principles and practice of Chemistry, ed 2, London, Hamilton & Adams 1871, pp.28-156, 489-494

12. Johnson CD: Medical and cardiological aspects of the passion and crucifixion of Jesus, the Christ, Bol Assoc Med PR 1987; pp.70: 97–102

13. Bloomquist ER: A doctor looks at crucifixion. Christian Herald, March 1964 pp 35, 46 – 48

14. The Crucifixion by personal friend of Jesus in to an Esseer Brother in Alexandria, Supplemental Harmonic Series vol II, 2nd ED, Chicago, Indo-American Book Co. 1907, pp.62, 64, 65

15. Lumpkin R: The Physical suffering of Christ, J Med Assoc Ala 1978; 47:8 – 10,47

16. Pfeiffer CF, Vos HF, Rea J (eds): Wycliff Bible Encyclopedia, Chicago, Moody Press, 1975, pp.149–152, 404–405, 713–723, 1173–1174, 1520–1523

17. Robertson AT: A Grammar of Greek New Testament in light of Historical Research, Nashville, Tenn, Broadman Press, 1931, pp.417–427

18. Kim H-S, Suzuki M, Lie JT, et al: Non-bacterial thrombotic endocadities (NBTE) and disseminated intervascular coagulation

(DIC): Autopsy study of 36 patients, Arch Pathol Lab Med 1977; 101 : pp.65–68

19. Becker AE, Van Mantgem J-P: Cardiac Tamponade: A study of 50 hearts. Eur J Cardiol 1975; 3: pp.349–358

20. Scott CT: A case of Haematidrosis, Br Med J 1918, pp

21. Boland, Barbara. "Pew Study: Christians Are The World's Most Oppressed." *cnsnews.com.* February 6, 2014, http://cnsnews.com/news/article/barbara-boland/pew-study-christians-are-world-s-most-oppressed-religious-group (accessed June 24, 2014).